love
Lists and
Labels

JEMMA SOLOMON

AKA THE LABEL LADY

EBURY
SPOTLIGHT

love
Lists and
Labels

MY TIPS FOR AN
ORGANISED LIFE
and CALM MIND

1 3 5 7 9 10 8 6 4 2

Ebury Spotlight, an imprint of Ebury Publishing
20 Vauxhall Bridge Road
London SW1V 2SA

Ebury Spotlight is part of the Penguin Random House group of companies
whose addresses can be found at global.penguinrandomhouse.com

First published by Ebury Spotlight in 2023
www.penguin.co.uk

A CIP catalogue record for this book is available from the British Library

ISBN 9781529910902
Printed and bound in Great Britain by Clays Ltd, Elcograf S.p.A.
Imported into the EEA by Penguin Random House Ireland,
Morrison Chambers, 32 Nassau Street, Dublin D02 YH68.

Penguin Random House is committed to a sustainable future
for our business, our readers and our planet. This book is made
from Forest Stewardship Council® certified paper.

To our children, Darcy, Mila and Hudson. While you are too young now to read and understand this book, I hope one day you read this and are proud of me. Everything is for you all and both Mummy and Daddy love you all more than you'll ever know.

Contents

Foreword

People are always asking me about myself; about my life, how I've got to where I am, where I started and whether the journey has been an easy one. (Simple answer – not always!)

So this seems like the perfect way to answer those questions properly and offer some insight into what I've learned along the way. I hope it will help other people explore their own lives and ambitions too – and also allow me to share my passion for lists and labels and how they can make a truly positive difference to your life.

It would be easy for me to gloss over certain things here, to present an 'Insta-perfect' view of my life and my journey to get to this point. But something that's really important to me is being honest about the hard bits too – partly because I want people to realise they are not alone in going through them, but also to show that you *can* get through them and come out the other side. That's exactly why I want to tell my story and inspire others to do something for themselves, whether it's a small change like organising part of their home (even a cupboard is a great start!), or something bigger such as starting a business of their own or following another long-held dream or ambition. People constantly say 'Thank you for showing me that I can do it too' and this means everything to me.

It began with a dream,
a want to do something,
a chance, a moment in
time and deciding to
do something I kept
thinking of but never had
the confidence to do!

I run my own business, I work full-time, I had three children at what's classed these days as a fairly young age ... it's fair to say my life is pretty busy, though I wouldn't change a thing. It's been hard at times but here I am.

I hope my experience will empower other people, especially women, and show them that they – yes you! – can do this too. You might have to work hard for it, but for me all the hard work has been totally worth it. I also want to encourage people to stick with their dreams and plans and not give up, because I know all too well that it can be tough. I haven't just had one job and then *bam!* here's my successful business. I've had several jobs. I've worked all the way through my pregnancies, through my maternity leave and there have been (very) many ups and downs. But I'm also proof that a normal person *can* do well and achieve what they want to. And if I can do it, so can you.

Empowering other women is a really important thing to do. For me, it's about making people feel like they have the ability to do something, no matter where they're from, who they are, where they are in their lives. It's about empowering people as individuals, not comparing with other people and what they might have achieved. So the aim of this book is not for you to read it and think, *Oh, but I'll never be Jemma or have my own business or anything like that*. It's about being yourself, becoming yourself and perhaps identifying with something here, something that I've done or I'm going through, and realising you can relate it to your own life – and then being empowered to make a change from that. It can be something small, like working out how to use a new dishwasher, or something big, like starting a company, or anything in between. It doesn't matter. It's about that 'feel-good factor' and feeling like you've achieved something.

> Sometimes the best person to take a chance on is yourself.

My book is about:

♡ | **LOVE**

And telling my story. Going behind the scenes
with my family – who have supported me as I
took a leap of faith towards my dreams – and
finding the people who will be there for me
no matter what. It's about learning to be true
to yourself, about following your instincts and
understanding your own worth.

▤ | **LISTS**

My passion! The process of ordering my
thoughts and making lists has been integral to
my life and I've found that it has been helpful
at each and every stage. I'll share practical
tips and takeaways, and I will show you that
listing can be fun (honest!) ... and equally, how
it has helped me to deal with anxiety and get
through some of the toughest times in my life.

▦ | **LABELS**

Not only my business but another thing that's
brought calm and order to my life. I'll look at
where to start and how to make the most of
organising your home and your life.

I hope *Love, Lists and Labels* will offer you:

💡 | INSPIRATION

To *be* yourself, to *believe* in yourself and to achieve whatever you set your mind to.

☆ | MOTIVATION

To make positive changes, be that at home, in business or other areas of your life, and to ride out the challenges on the way.

◈ | ORGANISATION

To show even if you start small, you can achieve big. Whether it's small-scale changes or bigger-picture ambitions, I believe that finding a sense of order is key.

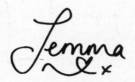

CHAPTER
ONE

Getting Started With the Rest of Your Life

 | |

It might have taken until my early thirties to find my true calling, but the foundations were laid at the very start by my family – my parents and siblings – and their values. Being there to boost each other, to support and build each other up has always been integral to all of our lives. We have never focused on who's done what or who has what, but on how we can uplift one another. For us, it's about how we've worked hard to achieve things in our own different areas and come together to celebrate those successes.

Be you, always

I'm the oldest of three, though my parents split up when I was ten and so I ended up with three step-siblings and a half sibling too, so there are seven of us in all. But in the early days it was just me, my sister and my brother and I have to admit I found being the oldest quite hard. I am sure that middle children and youngest children will disagree with me here, but being the first is not easy. I think the oldest child has the hardest job because they have to pave the way for everything. They're the ones who when they want to do something in life get told *no* because the parents almost have to get over the idea of their children doing whatever it is. Then the next one comes along and it's all, *yes, fine.* By the time they get to the third they're past caring!

I think I was quite a nice child. I was always quite arty-farty – some things never change. Some would say quite bossy (an eldest thing?!), definitely pretty clumsy, but never horrible. Looking back, I think that's where my leadership probably started, from being a first child. It's definitely influenced something along the way, that's for sure.

I was always close to my siblings, though when we were teenagers, my sister and I fought like cat and dog. There's only eighteen months between us so we were very much in that whole teen/hormonal stage at the same time. It's funny looking back because we are so close as adults, but back then ... definitely not! In fact, things got so bad that one day we got home from school to find my dad had built a wall down the middle of our bedroom to keep us apart. It wasn't ideal; it went right down the middle of the window and both halves were so small that you could literally just fit in a bed and a tiny desk. But it gave us our own space, which was a very good thing. As we matured, we put the bickering behind us and became friends, but in those days it really wasn't easy! We laugh about the fact that as we've got older we have found common interests. We both got really into organisation in different ways and now we love doing things like that together. That's not to say that there isn't still a healthy sibling rivalry. One example: Stacey has done these amazing Christmas doors for a couple of years. They really suit her house and look fantastic. I've never really got into it before but I've decided that next time I'm going to do it too ... and I'm going to do it better! It's typical sibling rivalry. We so want to discuss the designs, but secretly know we'll end up copying each other, so our lips remain sealed. We do laugh about it though!

But one thing about us, which I hope my own children will have too, is the fact that whatever we do, good or bad, we will always be there for each other through thick and thin.

The support of my family has been so key to everything in my life and I feel very lucky that my mum, dad, step-mum, brothers and sisters have always been behind me.

FINDING YOUR TRIBE

I realise that not everyone has the support of their family – but if you can find a couple of people who will always have your back and fight your corner, then that works every bit as well.

I think, for me, there are almost two sides to my support network and I've always tried to keep certain things separate. For example, I know my main group of friends will always offer emotional support and it's amazing to know that they are there for me. But generally I've always tried to have some detachment from my friends in terms of my working life. So if there is a problem on the business side of things, do I go to those friends? No. I like to see them because they're my friends and when I go out with them we have a great time. They help me let off steam and I don't want to muddy that by bringing work issues into a place which helps me decompress. So actually, they don't really know anything about what goes on inside the HQ or any daily stresses and struggles in that area. And I want to keep it that way because they're my fun people; we go out, we have a drink, we have a laugh. They're my escape. I do feel truly fortunate to have them in my life.

Before college, I had my secondary school friends but we drifted apart. To be honest, at school I wasn't the pretty one, I wasn't the popular one, I wasn't really anything. I liked school, though, and was very lucky that I was able to maintain a middle ground. It sounds stupid, but it can be a cruel place so I tried to get through it by being friends with everyone and using humour as a defence.

When I was in college (so around 16), I met a group of girls and we're all still close friends now. And while we don't see each other every day as we did in those days, when we were always partying, going on holidays, doing all the things that teenage girls do, I like to think we've got a kind of *Sex in the City* relationship where whenever we get together we know we can all offer that support to whichever of us needs it. Even within the group, we have mini support networks in different areas. We have our friends' WhatsApp group where we talk about anything and everything, and share our various ups and downs. We also have a mums' one too, because not all of them have kids and not everyone wants to hear what the babies are doing or what they're eating – or not eating – or what do to with teething and temperatures and rashes. So that's a separate thing again, where the mums of the group can discuss whatever they need to. Being a paediatric nurse, I get called upon probably once a week for various health niggles too. But it's all part of the give and take.

I'm so grateful to these girls, it feels like they've been there for me as long as I can remember. And I also have my best friend who I've been friends with since I was eleven and some other amazing friends that I've met over the years through work and when I was nursing. I count myself very lucky for all of them. It's funny – I'm not a hoarder and I have no problems getting rid of stuff. But people, that's a different thing altogether and I seem to want to keep them forever.

LEARNING FROM YOUR OWN EXPERIENCES

The support I've had from my family and friends has made me determined to ensure that my kids will have the same in their lives too. And even in the workplace, what I've been through myself has definitely influenced how I run The Label Lady, though in a very different way. The support I try to offer to my team now comes directly from the lack of support I received when I was working in the NHS. I really wanted to turn that around and not be that person. I wanted to be the supporter.

There are ten of us that work at the HQ and then my sister-in-law who lives in Switzerland and works remotely from there. So we have a WhatsApp group, which I think is really important, and I'll try and go and say hello to everyone every morning and check they're okay. I'll make sure I have catch ups with them, I'll do mini training sessions, I'll ask whether they think there's anything that needs improving or if there are things I could do better. It really matters to me that they are happy in what they're doing – they're a really nice bunch and I'm very lucky to have them all.

MUM AND DAD'S WORK ETHIC

This was imprinted on me from a young age and it's definitely served me well.

My dad would always say, 'I don't care what you do but you need to work and earn your crust', so I actually worked from the age of 14 – they were different times in those days! My best friend's nana had a nursery so I used to go every day for two hours after school and do the washing up in the kitchens. Sometimes I'd help with the dinner, making beans on toast or heating up shepherd's pie in the oven and dishing it out. And then after dinner I'd do the clearing up. I was there every single day and I loved it!

There were two nurseries so on some of the days I used to work with my friend which was an added bonus. And then in the summer holidays, I begged her nana to let me work as much as I possibly could, so I'd spend six hours a day washing up breakfast, lunch and dinner, sweeping and cleaning out the toy boxes. I think that was where I first learned the importance of never letting people down because they relied on me turning up each day. Something else that's stuck with me through the years.

I'd also grab extra shifts during my Christmas holidays and always took on Christmas temp jobs at our local shopping centre too. I worked in a gadget shop, a clothes shop and a shoe shop.

As I got a bit older, when I was finishing school, I started helping with the children at the nursery too and they put me in for my NVQ level 2 in childcare. Then, when I was at college doing my A levels, I carried on working there and did my level 3 NVQ. After that I got a job in a fish and chip shop with Stacey and then I worked at a wedding venue in Chigwell and we both ended up pulling pints there together as well. I worked all the way through school, college and uni too and because of that I've never been frightened of hard work. It's something I will definitely be passing on to my own kids.

Things are different now, of course, and it's not always so easy to find those sorts of jobs at that age, but the work ethic is something I will teach them no matter what. I want them to work to the best of their ability. Everyone has that spark in them somewhere, that thing that they're really good at, so it's about encouraging them to bring that out and helping them understand the benefits that working hard – in all areas of life – can bring.

There are certain things they don't teach in schools, such as looking after money, dealing with banks and so on, so it's important to me that they learn those sorts of things from us. At the grand ages of five, eight and ten, they already do little jobs to earn pocket money, which may sound trivial but I want to plant that seed now. To be honest, it doesn't matter whether you're mowing a neighbour's lawn for a fiver or doing a massive job search online and putting in a hundred applications, you have to start somewhere. It's about not procrastinating, but taking that step and moving forward.

When I was a kid I think we were very grounded. Everything was about family, we saw family all the time. That's how we grew up and it was great. But then I got to that point where I started to want other things in life as well. I was a typical teenager; *I want this, I want that*, and at that age you have no real concept of what things cost or how hard it is to get the money to pay for whatever it is you've set your heart on. I specifically remember everyone going mad for certain items of clothing; at one point they were all wearing these jackets which had this Velcro tab on them and you pulled the tab off, and the kids would swap them at school. I didn't have that coat, though I never felt hard done by. I never felt like I should have had it. I think my dad in particular has always said that these things are not important. He lost his dad when he was eleven, and knew first-hand no matter how expensive a pair of trainers was, he would have traded a hundred pairs to have had him in his life for longer. We just grew up and accepted it. We never felt like we were missing out as we knew our parents gave us lots of other things, so trivial items didn't matter.

But I did understand that if there was something I did really want then I had to go and find a way to pay for it myself. I think that's been instilled in us for ever. My dad always used to say to me, 'You can live with me for as long as you want but you also have to support yourself, you can't just be living off mum and dad', so I never expected them to pay for everything. I was very lucky, though, because right from the start they put all their energies into things like sending us on school trips and that was way more important than any jacket or pair of shoes or whatever was the current fad.

From the day I did that first shift at the nursery, I absolutely loved earning money of my own. I can still clearly remember getting my first pay cheque – about £160 for a whole month's work. It was when GHD straighteners had just come out and I had always had really curly frizzy hair so I really, really wanted them so I could have smooth, silky hair like everybody else. We were never given anything like that as children, like never, never, never. I told my mum and she wasn't happy, even though I was the one who was paying. She said, 'No, that's a whole month's money. Why would you do that? You can't spend all that.' But I wanted them so much that I bought them anyway, and I remember bringing them home and looking at my hair just all shiny and straight and it was worth every single penny – even if I did have no more money for the rest of the month.

I started working earlier than most of my friends, though in college a lot of them had jobs too. We didn't live in an affluent area – it was just a normal neighbourhood with normal people. We didn't have designer clothes or loads of holidays or anything but we always had what we needed. However, as I got older I wanted to do things and go places, so again, it was about earning the means to do that. I went on holiday with my friends at sixteen so I worked to pay for the flights and accommodation and my spending money, things like that. I probably worked too much, but I was hungry to earn so that was my choice. For me it was as much about being independent as the money I was earning, though I can't deny that I loved the money too!

I'm fortunate enough to have done amazing things and been to amazing places and knowing that I worked hard to get that made me all the more grateful for it. In my college days the travel agents would take monthly payments, so I used to go in each month and pay off a chunk of the holiday as soon as I got paid so I couldn't spend it. It's not so different from what I do now; if I look at a holiday and think, *I want that holiday*, I'll work hard and put money away so I can have that holiday. It's massively satisfying and you get a reward at the end of it!

FACING YOUR FEARS –
AND COMING OUT THE OTHER SIDE

I've always been more of a doer than an academic and have always enjoyed embracing my practical skills. I love using my hands and being creative. At school you do a bit with your hands but actually you've got to write a lot of essays and answer a lot of questions and do a lot of exams. It's the same at college and university. I'm much more about being able to do it and show you. Maths was the thing I struggled with the most, which was doubly hard because my siblings were *really* good at it. My mum thinks I was taught in a slightly different way, and perhaps I was, but any which way, it left me with a genuine fear of numbers.

You know when you make up a complex password and it's a whole series of numbers and letters? I'll be reading it out to my mum, who works with me now, and I'm absolutely convinced I've read it right, but she will say, 'It doesn't actually say that, Jemma, read what it says'. So in school I would do the essays and the other stuff but that fear of numbers would always be lurking. I didn't do science GCSE because of my fear of it, which is ironic given I later became a nurse, but obviously I had no idea I was going to follow that path at the time. In fact I remember going home and saying to my mum and dad, 'I need to pass maths – that's essential. But what am I going to use science for? Nothing.' (So naïve!) And I thought I could just learn what I need in life. So we went to the school and told them I wasn't doing it so I could concentrate on the maths, and I spent any extra time with my textiles teacher because I loved her – and of course that was a 'doing' subject too. I ended up with a C in maths, which might not be very good to some people but to me was absolutely amazing because I was so convinced I was going to fail it. It definitely wasn't easy to get to that point but I got through it and surpassed my expectations.

While I was at college I did my NVQs; they were also 'doing' ones, which was great for me. I had teachers who would come in and basically go through the paperwork with me, which helped hugely. I got through them and passed all my A levels, but I'm not going to lie; I spent most of my college life having fun. It was about friendships for me, about having the time of my life, and I didn't get great marks. I'd made peace with not being the pretty or popular girl, but being the funny friend paid dividends and meant I had a great relationship with the boys and the girls and mixed in so many circles.

I did get so upset about maths, though, that I'd end up crying. I just didn't get it and I didn't know why. After college, I didn't go straight to uni; I started working full-time instead. When I did go, three years later, there was that dread again. It also meant that as a nurse I was always extra careful because that genuine fear of numbers was always there. In fact, it almost cost me my first nursing job before I even began.

You had to pass a maths test to get through to the interview. And I failed it – not because I couldn't do it: I'd just passed three years of university and there was nothing more taxing than what I'd done while I was there. It was because of my fear. And also the test was frustrating because instead of giving you a drugs chart and getting you to do calculations for dosing children using that, which would have demonstrated the practical skills you would need for the role, it was all, *Jim went to the shops and bought eighteen oranges and a banana. How many drugs does Peter need?* And my brain just doesn't work like that. So I failed. But the person running it all came into the room and said to me, 'You're not failing this exam! You're working for me whether you like it or not.' And she ripped it up in front of me and said 'We're not speaking about this again'. Then she read through all the questions out loud but without the mumbo jumbo around them. And good on her, because then it all made complete sense to me and it showed me a different way to tackle it in future. I had let the numbers overtake me, and if it hadn't been for the manager believing in me and knowing I deserved a second chance, I don't know what would have happened. When I did that exam again I passed with flying colours and went through to the interview, and I was absolutely fine in that; put me in a million interviews and I'll talk till the cows come home. And then I did get the job because she knew I would be a bloody good nurse despite what that first piece of paper said and I respected her greatly for that.

So once again, I got through it in the end despite everything and the plus side was that it ensured that I was always incredibly careful; you can ask anyone I've ever nursed with but they would all tell you that I would constantly drive them crazy making 100 per cent sure I gave the right dose to the right child. We had what were known as the 'six Rs' to follow (right patient, right medicine, right route, right dose, right time, right documentation) and any time I was even a tiny bit unsure I checked that drug and never, ever made an error with any medication. And maybe sometimes it drove people up the wall a bit, thinking, *Oh my God, she's checking with me again*. But I didn't care because I would rather check a million times and know that I've done it right. It didn't mean I wasn't a good nurse, but simply that I knew that was my weakness and I had to overcome it.

I think a lesson you can take from that is that you should never, ever have preconceived ideas of people based on what they look like, what they sound like, their age or anything else. You should never think, *Oh, she's not great at maths so she can't do this*, or *You're not good at that so you can't do the other*. Maybe that person just needs to be guided or maybe they just need to be given an opportunity. I think so many jobs are decided by what's written on a piece of paper, which is ridiculous. When I started interviewing for a management role, they said to me, 'Oh, you didn't score high enough on the test paper.' I was like, 'Um, I've been doing the job for four months already and you're perfectly happy with how I'm doing the job.' And they still said, 'But the paper says you haven't scored high enough.' It was real 'computer says no' stuff. It drives me crazy!

It's funny, I was chatting with some of the girls at the HQ at lunch not long ago and we were talking about age and one of them said she was fifty-four. I was really surprised. I asked, 'Are you really fifty-four?' And she said, 'Jemma, you hired me! Didn't you look at how old I was?' And I said, 'No, I didn't even bat an eyelid about how old you were. You came in, I liked you and I couldn't care less. It's about the person, not the paper. What's important is can you do the job? Are you a nice person? Will you fit in here?' And yet ageism in the workplace is rife and it's still almost impossible to get a corporate job over the age of fifty. It's absolutely mad.

Has my fear of numbers impacted on me running a business? I haven't allowed it to stop me, even though I might spend *quite* a lot of time asking my accountants question after question! There's many a message where I'm asking to check if I can do this or buy that or order that stock, like my cold cups and storage jars and so on. Obviously I work it all out for myself first, but that reassurance from them is really helpful to me. A lovely guy called Andrew taught me how to make specific spreadsheets for buying and selling and all the different formulas that go with it. And when I first looked at it I was like, *Whoa, I haven't done anything like this since IT GCSE* (and I probably should have listened a little bit harder when I was doing it) so I had to teach myself again. Andrew went over it with me and set up a template and told me to make one for my business and I had to do it. It was all good, but even so, again I always, always, always check everything because I never want to get into trouble or do anything wrong. So basically I will do it all and then send it to my accountant saying, 'Please can you check this?' It's okay to ask for help!

And there's another thing. Never assume that people who appear confident know what they're doing. If I think back to my time working in the hospital, as a nurse there were certain things I was allowed to write out, such as blood-transfusion prescriptions and so on. These had to be signed by a doctor. I would write the whole thing out and sometimes they would sign it without a second glance and off they'd go. And I'd say, 'Uh-uh, come back, now add it up and make sure I've done it right. Just because I write it doesn't mean I'm right.' Always check and have the confidence to ask those questions. It's easy to agree just because someone says it's okay. At uni they always taught us that whatever decision you make, you need to be confident that you would be happy to back it up in a court of law, and that's stuck with me always.

I think the way I've always coped with it is by assuming it's wrong – I've already got that negative inside myself.

I associate myself with being bad at this and bad at that. So the checking everything is always there even now. I wish I'd found a way to deal with it when I was younger, but I didn't, so now it's about how I manage it.

That means I'm the same with the labels, and getting the girls to check them. I say, 'It doesn't matter if I'm the boss. Sometimes I'm working seventeen-hour days, I'm going to make mistakes.' Just because you appear confident doesn't mean you're infallible.

It's important to me to know what the point of things is. So when I was nursing, if I was using a drug I would want to know how that drug would act and what it would do. Because then I would know exactly what to look for when I checked on the patient. More recently, when I wanted to make my minimalistic labels waterproof and wipe-proof and so on, I needed to understand how that process worked, how did it do that, why did it do that, what would happen if I scratched it. It needs to sit right in my brain before I can move forward with it. It's important to remember that we all process things in different ways and that doing things differently should never be an issue if it gets you there in the end. It's all about learning your craft.

LIFE LESSONS

One of the things I'm most grateful to my parents for was them making me feel I could go out and achieve anything I set my mind to (even with my fear of numbers!) My dad used to talk to me about computers. When I grew up we had dial-up internet – this makes my kids laugh at me, because I think I'm young – and they definitely weren't the super sophisticated machines we have now, but even then I remember him telling me there are two things to remember. First of all, if you get a new piece of equipment or you want to do something in life or you're trying something new then you have to really give it a go. You have to turn that machine on or press those buttons, or you do whatever you need to until you know what you're doing. You have to think, *What's the worst that could happen?* And as long as you're not harming anybody you just get on with it. So he'd be like, 'you want to learn how to use that computer? Press those buttons, click those things and if it goes wrong you'll find someone who can fix it'. And it made me realize that that works in pretty much every part of my life too. If I was starting a new job, for example, and I didn't know how things worked, I'd just go for it; I'd ask all the questions, say, 'Tell me what I need to be doing and I'll do it'. And I figured, what's the worst that can happen? I might do it wrong but I will learn to do it right next time. So even now I refer back to that computer scenario and I use that in my life quite a lot.

IT'S OKAY TO SAY NO

The other thing Dad always said to me was 'Don't make promises you can't keep.' I think that stands for a lot when you're trying to achieve things, because much as you might want to do whatever is asked of you, you can't say yes to everything. There comes a point where you have to say no or you have to ask for help. Being able to do that is sometimes really difficult, but otherwise you can end up completely overfacing yourself, promising all these things that you simply don't have time to do, then letting down a whole array of people, which can have a humungous knock-on effect, and you're just one part of it. So be realistic about what you can do and don't say yes when you know it's just not going to be possible. Those are the two principles I always try to stick to.

I've already mentioned the unwavering support I've had from my family but while I've always known they will be there for me, that's in terms of encouragement and moral support rather than picking up the pieces if I ever made a massive mistake financially. I didn't have a daddy sitting at home with his bank account saying, 'Don't worry, darling, I'll press a few buttons and send over a few thousand'. It's never been like that, but I'm glad I was taught to stand on my own two feet. Again, it's a great life lesson.

Talking of life lessons ... when I was 17 I passed my driving test first time. It was a 'doing' thing and I sailed through it. However, a week later I wrote off my first car and that feeling of being an invincible teenager came to a swift end. It's funny how you feel no worries at that age. I sometimes miss that feeling of being young and carefree.

I think whether it's a job or a hobby or a business, when it comes to following your chosen path it's great to find that inner confidence that my family helped to instil in me. Some other things that have proved really useful to me at different times are:

- ✓ **NETWORKING.** I think this is one of the best things you can do, especially in this day and age. You don't necessarily have to do it face to face. I work with Dell, for example, and they have an entrepreneur network online. There are plenty of other ways to network too, and you don't have to show your face if that's not your bag; you can tap into things like forums, and Facebook groups, both of which are great for meeting like-minded people with shared interests or goals. Whether you're looking to develop a business or take up a hobby or activity, talking to other people is a great way to start. You might say, *I've done this so far, what next? Or is there a better way to do that? Where can I find ... how do I ... ?* and so on. Online groups can be really useful, though I think there is definitely value in trying to attend in-person events too. Recently, for example, there was an event at Excel in London, a Clean and Tidy show, so I went along and found a whole wealth of community in the area of cleaning and organising. So if you're thinking, *I really want to do this but am not sure where to start*, that sort of thing is the perfect place to visit. Obviously to go somewhere in person and meet and talk to people you don't know requires a bit more confidence. If that's not for you, then stick to online networking where you can hide a little bit of yourself behind the screen.

⊘ USING SOCIAL MEDIA. We are all aware that there are pros and cons to any sort of online activity and you've got to be able to switch off from the not so nice sides. But there is also a lot of positivity that can come from it. I think unless we push the positive side of social media and teach people to look for that rather than the bad side then we can lose what is there as a constructive resource. I've had many really positive experiences so I choose to focus on those.

☑ **FINDING THE INFORMATION I NEED** wherever I can. Talking to other people is super useful, but in addition, Google is a godsend and books are great too. Even if you're not a big reader, pick out parts of books that will help you. You don't have to plough through the whole thing.

ORGANISATION IS KEY!

Part of working hard for me has always involved organisation. I find it difficult to do things without having everything in place and I was like that even when I was very young too.

As a child, I had one of those high beds with the desk underneath. And I remember, even then, I had all of my own little pots where I'd put all of the different pens and pencils and rubbers and all of that sort of stuff, and I'd have all my drawers laid out too. I think it's probably in the blood; I remember our mum organising the Lego, literally into people, flowers, objects, colours, everything. The kitchen cupboards would have certain spaces with crisps in one, biscuits in another and so on. Not labelled and organised in the way I do now but very much using the same mentality. So we always had that around us and I think it must have been instilled in us subconsciously, and then it came out as we got older. Even in school and college, I was the one who liked organising things and all these years later, the girls will be like, *Jemma, party at yours for Christmas?* Because I like to be that person with a plan and lots of lists, I've always been the person they come to to say, 'Right, you can run that' or 'You can organise that' or whatever. I love it!

Being organised is a brilliantly practical skill in just about all areas of life. It might seem daunting if you're faced with a mess or loads of clutter or a million things to do (there's lots more on that in chapter four), but taking a step back and sorting out a plan not only saves time there and then, but also makes life much easier going forward. Any time spent organising is a brilliant investment in my book!

CHAPTER TWO

The Life-Changing Magic of Lists

I've been big into lists since I was a child. My favourite time of year was when we would go back to school at the end of the six-week holiday. Why? Because I'd get a new pencil case with new pens and pencils. I'd put together lists of what I would put in my pencil case, lists of what would come to school with me. And when I was at secondary school and we had to cover all our books in wrapping paper – I loved it – that activity went on the lists too and I was in my element. People have often asked when all this started for me and I'm like 'Oh my gosh, remember I used to do all that when I was really young?' So I guess I feel like it's just something I've always done; I've never actually thought it was anything different from what I should be doing really.

So yes, the bottom line is that I love lists and I always have. They are EVERYWHERE in our house and now I watch my daughter Mila do the same and I think, *My work here is done.* I remember when we moved the business from the den in our garden to our new HQ and I had lists of things we needed to buy, lists of where things were going to go, lists of what I was going to do. They were in the shed, they were in the HQ, they were in our bedroom – poor Lee didn't know which one to follow. But joking aside, they really are the perfect way to get things out of your head and help you switch off without forgetting all the stuff you need to remember. (And there always seems to be SO much stuff to remember!)

THE JOY OF LISTS

Where do I start?! They don't just make life easier but they can even bring enjoyment in their own right. Writing things down, highlighting them, ticking them off or drawing little stars next to them. (I'm a doodler so mine have plenty of those on too.) They bring order, satisfaction and they can have aesthetic appeal too! That's a win in my book.

People have always commented on how neat my handwriting is. That's not only a plus for listing, but has also proved useful because as well as struggling with numbers, I've had real issues with spelling too; I've found over the years that my brain will read a word but doesn't process how it's spelled. I've even tried going back to basics and doing the children's spelling tests with them, but my brain just doesn't retain the information. I often get pulled up on it on Instagram, but I've also learned to live with it. I've got through school, college and university and while my spelling may not be the best, that obviously doesn't make me a bad person or mean I'm not good at my job. Having good handwriting has always been helpful to me, though, and this really came into its own when I was nursing; I was taught from the very start that your notes are your protection. Anything that happens, write it up so that if needed the records are all there, clear and accurate. My colleagues used to laugh because the doctor would make notes and no one could read them, we'd have the magnifying glass out trying to decipher the writing. And then they'd get to mine and they'd say, 'Ah, now we know everything that's happened to the patient because the writing is so beautiful. But the words ... the spelling of these words is hilarious.' But they didn't care about that so much because they knew 100 per cent what it was saying.

Handwriting apart, I actually find making lists look good really satisfying. The process of putting them together is more enjoyable when they are visually appealing, plus it's the perfect excuse to invest in list-making stationery. There's nothing I love more than a set of gel pens or highlighters in all different shades. It's a real feel-good experience.

And I love the way they work too, by lifting weight from your brain. We all work so hard; I don't necessarily mean in business or however you earn a living, but life generally can get pretty hectic. What you want to find is that moment of serenity, and writing things down and being able to tick them off gives you that calm space, even if it's just for a few minutes. That's still a few minutes that you don't have to juggle all those thoughts in your head.

WHAT ARE LISTS GOOD FOR?
ABSOLUTELY EVERYTHING!

You might be running a sports team, or teaching classes. You might be organising family life or planning a holiday. Perhaps you have a busy job, have presents to choose, things to do for the home – whatever you're trying to achieve, lists are handy for pretty much every scenario.

> Lists are about what makes your life tick (in every sense). They don't just have to be about shopping!

WHY LISTS WORK

Think of all the information you have flying around your brain which is constantly jumbled around. It can be hard to make sense of it all, let alone remember all the many things you need to. But when you write it down, suddenly you have an instant visual aid right in front of you. Not only a visual of what you have to do – and yes, sometimes this can be overwhelming – but also a visual of what you will have accomplished once you've ticked everything off. Taking all that information out of your brain and dumping it on a piece of paper helps immediately in my opinion. The act of writing things down also reinforces them without the stress of having to juggle umpteen different things in your mind. And when it is all down in front of you, you can then be more pragmatic with it too. Your first list might end up fairly humungous as you pull everything out of your head onto the paper, but then that gives you the chance to examine it more easily so you can organise it further from there.

Then you say to yourself, okay, there are only seven days in a week and so there's only so much I can do in a given time frame. So if you give yourself a certain number of tasks a week or a day or whatever you have time for, you can start crossing things off and already your brain will feel just a tiny bit lighter. Lists are basically a release, a way of taking things off the weight of your brain.

HOW TO MAKE A LIST

Theoretically making a list is the simplest thing going. Grab a bit of paper, and then jot down all the things you need to remember to do/buy/go to, etc.

But organising your lists effectively can make a massive difference, both in seeing what needs to be done and also what's already been crossed off. It's much harder to mark your progress on a long and rambling list where everything is jammed in together and in no particular order at all.

That said, splurging everything out onto a piece of paper is a great way to start the process. I think of it as a brain unscramble. It can be quite daunting if you haven't done it before, but it doesn't have to have any form or structure at this point (this is not your actual list, it's about getting everything out so it's really just the first step). So spend ten minutes (or however long you need) writing down your thoughts; basically just go for it and get it all down. Don't worry about making it neat or finding any sense of order for this bit. It's simply about getting all the stuff that's flying round your brain out before you can turn it into a proper list, otherwise it's like, *What am I listing? I'm thinking about so much right now and I don't know what that is.* (Sometimes you will look at your piece of paper and wonder, why am I even thinking about that?) Getting it out is all part of the process. Don't be afraid of what comes out, and remember that this part doesn't all have to be doing things or actions such as shopping. It can be thoughts about how your day has gone, anything that's playing on your mind or part of the internal scramble – those can also work in terms of putting together your final list. So if you've put that you feel tired and anxious, then that could prompt a list of self-care activities. Any which way, get it out and you'll have clear space in your brain that will allow you to take on new challenges.

Splurging everything out onto a piece of paper is a great way to start the process. I think of it as a brain unscramble.

BRAIN UNSCRAMBLE

Clear space in your brain to allow yourself to feel ready for new challenges

Your thoughts are your own. This is for you so don't be afraid of what might come out.

It could be a date that plays on your mind ...

'Last day of term 20th December!'

It doesn't have to be a doing thought e.g. *'need to go shopping'*. It can be a thought of how your day went

WRITE IT ALL DOWN

Sometimes the hardest thing is working out what's the most important thing! Write down everything that's in your mind, all in one go, then you can use this to regroup and make the most productive lists.

You can look back on your thoughts as a way to see what you have achieved!

There may be thooughts that are feelings ... if you have a feeling, this can turn into a list

'I feel ...
– tired
– anxious'

Seeing your thoughts allows you to see a visual, giving you a push to taking action

SELF CARE
* Read a book this week
* Watch a movie
*Get my nails done

The next step is about organising it into something more manageable and breaking it down into sections. Look at your unscramble page and identify common themes. You might use a spider graph or grab some highlighters so you can differentiate between the various areas. So, for example, anything to do with home might be in green so that becomes the green list, anything highlighted in pink is family and becomes the pink list and so on.

The main thing here is to look at what you've written down and distil it into two or three areas (or more if needed). For example, here I'm worried about the garden, here I'm worried about the kids, school dinners, after school activities, and here I need to think about the house, and so on. So then you can create those three separate sections – or as many as you want – and move things as appropriate. So whether it's home, shopping, family or whatever, split the things accordingly. Once you've done that it will already start to feel more manageable.

Then it's time for your **HEADLINES**. If, say, you're about to go on holiday, these might be things like:

THINGS TO BUY

THINGS TO WASH/CLEAN

THINGS TO PACK

THINGS TO DO BEFORE WE GO

And then under each headline add appropriate points, for example:

THINGS TO BUY
* Sun cream
* Insect repellent
* Rehydration sachets
* New flip flops (etc.)

THINGS TO WASH/CLEAN
* Beach towels
* Buckets and spades from shed
* Swimwear (etc.)

THINGS TO PACK
* Sunglasses
* Chargers
* Adaptors
* Passports (etc.)

THINGS TO DO BEFORE WE GO
* Leave note for milkman
* Cancel newspapers
* Arrange for next door to feed the fish/gerbils/rabbit
* Put a loaf in the freezer for when we get back
* Exchange currency (etc.)

Another good way to sort lists is by splitting things into priorities or non-priorities (or urgent/less urgent or important/less important). Then you can see at a glance what needs to be done first if you don't have time to do everything in one go.

Prioritising is super important and this is where lists come in to their own. If you've got a lot of stress on because you've got a massive birthday party to plan, why are you ticking off the ironing or tidying the shed? Why are you panicking about cooking a turkey dinner when that's three weeks away and you have twenty things that need to be done before that? You need to work on what's at the front of your brain and what's causing you the most angst so you can achieve it, move it out of the way and move on to the next thing. As you do this, you will start to realise, hang on, that's a really important thing that *will* affect me and my life and that thing isn't so important and it *isn't* going to affect me, so it can wait. Sometimes we get consumed by things that aren't actually going to affect us, but we get so caught up by outside influences or what's going on in the world or what's happening around us that we think they're the most important things, when actually they aren't at all and they're pretty small in comparison to everything else. That's why putting everything down on paper and having it in front of you gives you that time and space to reflect on what matters most and what you really need to be doing first.

When you're sorting out priorities, it's also important to remember to set realistic time frames. Life, work, children, pets are all factors and they all take up time. Now you need to make time for you to do the things you need too.

⊘ **USE YOUR CALENDAR.** We happily write down play dates or work meetings, so do the same for the jobs on your list. It's a great way to carve out time to get things done.

⊘ **DON'T OVER-COMPLICATE YOUR LIST.** Try to stick to a maximum of six points, making sure the things that need doing first are at the top. Anything else can go on another – less urgent – list to be moved up as and when.

The most satisfying thing in the world is crossing things off a list when you've done them. In fact, sometimes I make lists just to be able to tick things off. Just for fun. If you've had a stressful day, try writing down everything you've done then tick them all off. Feels good and also helps stop everything that's gone on swirling around your brain all evening. *Done, ticked off, relax.* Clearing and freeing your brain is the most important part of all of this.

Like anything else, different ways of listing will work for different people. Some like things day or date ordered, whereas I actually struggle with the whole diary thing, the whole Monday, Tuesday, Wednesday, Thursday ... because

I find it quite regimented and my life is not regimented at all – anything but. One minute I'll be here and then there will be a phone call and I've got to be over there. We already have a diary for work, with meetings and things to do, one for events and outings or appointments for the children and so on, so having a to-do list that is set in stone to add to all that is something I find difficult, though I know others like the idea of knowing what they need to do when. Different strokes, as they say. I work best with a complete list of everything I need to get done and then I can look in my diary and work out the spaces to fit things in as needed. We use our diaries for everything else in our lives, so why not use it to block out time to achieve something for you, or get on top of things on your list? So you might have an hour between a Zoom call and school pick-up, so put that in as the time to do your holiday list (or your supermarket shop or send those emails and so on).

When it comes to the order of doing things that have similar time priorities, of course it would be easy just to do all the small things first so you can then tick them all off. But actually, I find it can be really satisfying to do it the other way round. This is how I work when I'm at the HQ. So I might get an order with just one label on it. Or I might get an order with several pages of labels on it. And as I say to the girls in the office, you have to look at what you want to achieve here. Are you in a hurry? Is this something you need to do quickly or have you got all day to do it? If you've got the whole day then it can be good to get the big or more complicated order done in the morning, while your brain is at its freshest. Then it's done and out of the way; you can relax a bit and then you can fly through the smaller orders in no time at all, tick, tick, tick. You get a real sense of achievement and you know you only have smaller bits and bobs left to do rather than a massive thing to complete.

Occasionally it can work better the other way round. I might have a big order with a mix of files or colours that takes for ever to do and a busy day where I'm short of time and don't have the opportunity to do a longer task until later on. Then it's good to do the little ones, give yourself that little boost. So I will fit those smaller things on the list around everything else and have the satisfaction of at least being able to tick those off while I carve out a block of time for the larger project. I find it's great to know you've cleared all the small ones, when you've done, say, fifty orders and then there is only one thing on the list left to do. But mostly I like to tackle the bigger things first and get the heavy stuff out of the way and then you can just fly through the rest.

Grab some highlighters! They brighten all lists!

BREAKDOWN OF HOW TO WRITE A LIST

1. **BRAIN UNSCRAMBLE.** This part isn't about order, it's about creating a visual. When you can see something in front of you, it's easier to pull it apart. List out any:

   Thoughts

   Feelings

   Things to do

   Things on your mind (big or small)

2. **USE YOUR BRAIN UNSCRAMBLE TO CREATE CATEGORIES.** Don't worry if you have lots – that's where step three takes over.

3. **TIME TO PRIORITISE.** Sometimes the reason we feel like we are not achieving things is because it all feels overwhelming. Now it's time to look at your categories and decide what's most important.

   What will lift the biggest weight?

   What will make you feel good?

   Remember your lists are for you. The biggest thing you can do is complete them in the order that helps your life, not in the way you see others doing on social media.

4. **NOW WE LIST!**

MANAGING YOUR TIME EFFECTIVELY

Family, kids, relationship, home, skating, life, the business ... I'm often asked how I fit it all in. Lists play a huge role in the way I organise everything – of course – but really learning to manage my time has also been absolutely key. It's impossible for me to do all the things I need to in a Monday to Friday, nine to five kind of way, so again it's about identifying priorities. Also accepting that you can't do absolutely everything at the same time (however much you might want to!)

I think a lot of my understanding of this comes from my hospital days because whenever I went on shift I would have no idea what I was going to have to do in that 12-hour period. It was a really high turnover general paediatric department, everything from children with broken bones to those who were critically ill, and until I got there on any given day I wouldn't know how many patients there would be, how they would be allocated, what their needs and requirements were. Planning ahead was impossible and I had no choice but to learn to time-manage on the day. This has definitely helped me approach life now, though; I'll walk into the HQ and see what needs to be done today, then manage that without thinking too far ahead. When you're constantly looking at what's in the future it's all too easy to lose sight of the here and now. It's all about putting the most important stuff at the front and focusing on that.

The girls have skating four times a week and on three of those days we have to be at the rink by 6.20 in the morning. Do you think I make the beds before we go? I absolutely do not! It's just not important in the scheme of things. What matters at that point is that we get out of the door and get to the rink on time. And then it's straight back home afterwards, kids get changed, eat breakfast and off to school, so again the beds don't get a look in. I know it's important to some people that beds are made first thing because it makes them feel better, but the reality for me is that if I want to get four beds made in that 6 a.m. morning rush it's only going to add to the stress – so I don't do it. I have enough going on at that point and stressing myself out with things that aren't essential isn't going to help. Yes, in the perfect Instagram house all the beds are neatly made and the curtains are drawn back and whatever but that's a situation that doesn't work for me and there's no way I'm getting up half an hour earlier to make it happen. It's frantic enough as it is! Mila doesn't love getting ready in the mornings, though once we're at the rink she's completely fine and whizzing around so I find ways to make it easier, not harder, for both of us. I save a few minutes by dressing her the night before. Shower, into her skating clothes, she sleeps in them – it's not like kids get dirty when they're asleep – and it's one less thing to do in the morning. No different from a mum doing the school run in her pyjamas, and I think a lot of us can hold our hands up to that one.

Build the stuff that you know has to be done into your routine and deal with other things that come up around this. If something's urgent, try to get it done as soon as you can so it's not hanging over you. If it's not, then stick it on the list so you know you need to make time for it and you don't forget or stress about trying to remember it. The oven might need cleaning, for example, but getting the kids up and dressed, teeth brushed and to school on time has to come first. If it's on the list you can block out time to do it as soon as you have the chance. Likewise, if a message or an email comes through, try not to leave it lingering – if it's something that can be replied to with a quick or simple answer, try to do it there and then. Sometimes just answering at that point means the question isn't left to crowd your brain; it's gone and out of the way before it had the chance! And what's more, it's likely to be really helpful on the receiving end too.

It's important to remember that there are no rights and wrongs here; it's all about finding out what formats and methods work for you as an individual. One thing I will say, though, is keep your lists as succinct as you can! I much prefer to have things that are short, sharp and to the point in front of me than pages and pages of stuff which, let's be honest, you're never going to go back and read. So I do think it really pays to be concise and focused.

Of course, there is no point in making a list if you're then just going to ignore it. So it's essential you make sure you put it where you can see it. I usually have my lists on my desk where they're right in front of me. Or at home on the fridge. Somewhere where you can't miss them is what to aim for.

WHEN TO LIST

Obviously the simple answer to this is whenever you need to. So with this in mind, it's good to have your listing equipment handy at all times. For example, I find that sometimes after a busy day I will sit down to watch TV in the evening and I can't concentrate because my head is buzzing and my brain is thinking about anything and everything, so I keep a pad and pen on a side table next to the lamp and I can just jot things down on there. I've found it really helpful. If you're the kind of person who gets into bed and then finds a million thoughts swirling around and keeping you awake, a pen and paper by your bedside is great too. Get it out of your head, onto the paper and then sweet dreams.

(A word of warning, though: it's definitely best to do this *before* you go to sleep, as if you wake up in the middle of the night and try jotting things down then, your handwriting may not be at its best.

It's absolutely useful to have your pen and paper there on these occasions as it means you can write whatever it is you need to remember, turn over and go back to sleep with a clear head. But bear in mind that I have a friend who spent days trying to work out what 'reply give descript otter' meant before giving up altogether!)

P.S. – BEWARE!

If you find yourself with more lists than you know what to do with, it's because you're not using your lists properly. Just writing them is not enough. Otherwise what are you achieving? Answer: you're not achieving anything. You're just writing and writing and writing and not actually doing anything about them. So you have to be motivated and action what you're writing. That's why it's important to break them down into categories and pick out the things you're going to do first as your week unfolds.

LISTING FOR LIFE EVENTS

Having a baby, planning a wedding, moving house ... these are times lists come into their own more than ever. There's so much involved that having that organisation and focus is absolutely key.

If you're moving house, you might have lists for things to pack (knowing that you might not get to those boxes any time soon), things that need to be unpacked as soon as you arrive, things that you will need at the new place, things to get rid of before the big day and so on. Keeping a list of what's in each numbered box is invaluable. Oh and make sure your list of things to take with you (rather than in the van) includes a kettle, mugs, tea bags, milk and biscuits!

For a new baby you might have a list of things you need to buy, things to go in the hospital bag, things you need to do or prepare before the birth. Having those in front of you and seeing what's been ticked off and what still needs to be done is so useful at such a busy time, when you're often trying to tie things up at work as well as attending hospital appointments on top of everything else.

Lists are also great for planning hen nights and baby showers – I did both for my sister – and especially for weddings, where there is SO much that needs doing to make the day run smoothly.

I planned a lot of my sister's wedding, like a lot, which was ... well, let's say interesting because our methods of doing things are at the opposite ends of the scale. I like to start planning things as many months in advance as possible, whereas she'll literally be like, 'Oh hi, can we have a marching band in my garden tomorrow?' We're very different like that.

So it came to the time, and I kid you not, three days before she was like, 'I need some extra tables because I've got these extra guests'. I said, 'I'm not sure that will be possible because the tables are being brought in. It's not a venue where you can just turn up and they'll put up a few extras.' I did get it sorted, even though it meant adjusting the table plan, which had taken hours and hours of working out where everyone needed to be. But still, all done. We had those cards with names on that guests could pick up to find their table numbers and laid them out alphabetically. They looked great ... until the bloody wind blew them away. The whole lot of them. So after the ceremony and the drinks reception everyone came down waiting to be seated and I had no idea who some of the people from work and so on were. I decided the only solution was for me to be the table plan in human form and lead everyone to their seats instead. It ended up that I sat everyone in that entire wedding down and made them comfortable ... and then realised I'd forgotten about myself! I had no seat, though I obviously wasn't going to say anything, so I sat on Lee's lap. But it also meant I had no plate, no place setting. And when we went up for the buffet I had nothing to put my food on – so I used a flower pot!

The wedding had been delayed because of Covid, so we only had four or five months in the end once the date was finalised. Although therein lies a funny story. I had the date in my diary, all the suppliers had the dates in their diaries. And Stacey and Joe? Had written it in for a week later! Luckily I found out in time to set them straight.

I was maid of honour so I organised the bridesmaids, and also helped organise the suppliers and the overall plan for how everything was going to work. I love planning things like this because there's always a fun party at the end of the day, and the listing and listing all pays off.

If you find yourself planning a wedding or occasion for someone else, here are a few tips to make sure you're all still speaking at the end of it!

⊘ **BEWARE OF EMOTIONAL OVERLOAD.** Helping out a family member or close friend can be stressful because you care deeply for them, and sometimes you have to almost step into a non-emotional role, otherwise you can get overwhelmed by not wanting to upset them or not make something happen. Be open and honest and talk things through. And if there's something you're struggling with, let them know at the earliest time possible.

✓ **BE FIRM WITH OTHER PEOPLE.** If you're the maid of honour, for example, you'll find there's always someone who doesn't like the colour or doesn't want to wear a particular dress, or wants their hair a certain way. And in the end you have to turn round and say, 'This isn't your wedding, this isn't my wedding, you're privileged to have been asked to play such a close part in it. I'm in charge and what I say goes.' Otherwise it ends up with things getting out of control or the bride getting stressed – both of which you obviously want to avoid. This is super hard I know, especially when family and friends are involved. But I believe that the fact they are family/friends means they should understand that they are part of someone they care about's big day and sometimes we just have to smile and get on with it. However, nine times out of ten the bride will want nothing more than for her bridal party to be happy, so if you do decide to say something, it's all about how the situation is approached. Choose your words wisely!

✅ **SEPARATE THE DIFFERENT PARTS** – the actual wedding, the hen do, the bridesmaids, the dresses and so on – and have specific lists for each. Much less daunting (fewer tasks on each list) and saves things getting lost. The brain unscramble I described is perfect for sorting what goes where.

✅ And in terms of general organisation, whether planning for someone else or yourself, take time to **FILE ALL THE EMAILS** from suppliers, etc. It will save so much time when you need to check something. So make files for 'resolved' and 'outstanding', so you're almost erasing what you don't need as you go along, but can still refer back if you need to. And then folders for each thing, e.g. catering, furniture or decor, band or DJ and so on.

OTHER LISTING TIPS THAT I FIND USEFUL

☑ USE LISTS AS A WAY TO LEAVE WORK AT WORK and not bring it home with you. It's very simple; at the end of your working day, make a list of everything you still have left to do. That way, it's down on the paper and you can leave it at the door without it running through your head all evening – and you get to use that precious time to relax.

☑ KEEP A RUNNING LIST FOR GOING BACK TO SCHOOL. At the beginning of the summer holiday it's easy to get into no-school mode and avoid thinking about the start of term until it's almost upon you. And then suddenly all the stuff you need to remember seems really daunting. But if you have a list that you can add to over the holidays, then you can just jot stuff down as you go along and work through it gradually. No big stress at the start of September.

☑ LISTS DON'T JUST HAVE TO BE WORDS. You might have loads of things you want to do around your home. (These lists have a tendency to be never-ending so it's always worth first asking yourself if you're happy with the way things are. If you are, that's great. Don't put pressure on yourself to make everything 'Insta-perfect' because that's not real life.) Maybe there are things you want to do – say, a wall you want to add pictures to, a window that needs a new blind, a space that needs a piece of furniture or something that needs painting and so on. It's all too easy to keep brushing them aside because there will always be something else in life that requires your attention, or somewhere you need to be, or something that feels more important or whatever. Getting it all on paper and having that list will give you that proper vision of what you want to achieve. For things like this, an illustrated list can work brilliantly. It's a different way of pulling things together but it's every bit as effective. So you might screenshot something and print it off or rip something out of a magazine and add it to the page. You know when you spot things and think, *Oh that's nice* and then instantly forget where you saw it, so when it comes to it it's just a vague memory? This way, you have that visual reminder in front of you, to inspire you and make you think *hang on, I still really want to do X or Y*. I suppose it's a bit like a Pinterest board but one you can stick on your fridge and where you can tick things off as you go!

HIGH TECH LISTING

The day I discovered the thing on my phone which allows you to make lists and tick, tick, tick things off was one of the happiest days ever! It's super useful for making lists on the go. If you use Notes, you can even add a square to make a tick box. I've got tons of lists on my phone now and use them all the time.

It's a really useful tool for when you're out and about and don't have a pen and paper handy – again, it stops you having to retain everything in your brain until you get home. But ... I still don't think it is as efficient as writing everything down and having that physical list in front of you, so that will always be my go-to.

Wherever and whenever you make them, if you want to clear your brain, lists are everything, offering a sense of doing, completion, achievement, satisfaction and order. And all for free. You really can't argue with that.

Embracing the Juggle & Accepting the Drops

It would be fair to say that we didn't have the most conventional start to our family life, because when I got pregnant both Lee and I were living with our parents and so we spent our time going backwards and forwards between houses, though we ended up predominantly at my mum's. So the order that existed pre-children wasn't really ours but our parents' – and Lee's mum is VERY, VERY tidy, to the point where we had to have discussions because I would make the bed, and then she would remake it. And I had to say to her that if she was going to do that every time I left the house, I might as well have an extra twenty minutes in bed. But I love that he's inherited all that from his mum and I'm so glad I met someone who is as into it all as me!

When we did eventually buy a place, the completion date was when I was in hospital after having Darcy by emergency Caesarean section. So my whole family had to move house for us. I went into hospital from one house and went home to another. The family did everything for me while I recuperated from the birth ... they were amazing. But I'm a very independent person and so now, looking back, I think deep down I actually found that difficult and that it played a part in my loss of control (more on that and my anxiety in chapter five)

You might be the tidiest, most organised person on this earth but having kids is almost guaranteed to upset that equilibrium. I found it really hard.

I love organising, though I don't really like cleaning, and obviously the two sort of go hand in hand. You don't want to be organising in a dirty space. And I really did not want to clean when I had Darcy, I just didn't. So essentially what happened was that everything started to spiral backwards and sometimes you can only go so far backwards before you find yourself thinking, *Where do I start?* and having to go back to the beginning.

But as I always say to people, the thing you forget is that a newborn baby is not messy! They don't do anything, they're just laying there. It's all the stuff that goes with them. So it was more the fact we weren't washing-up the bottles straight away or throwing the bin bag out or whatever needed doing. And I really struggled with that. Lee's always been a really good cleaner, but obviously he went back to work and when he got home there was only so much he could do. So it was really hard for me to come to terms with the changes and I struggled with finding my mojo again.

And as if that's not enough, when they become toddlers it's a whole different ball game. All the toys and stuff everywhere and they really do make a mess. That's hard to deal with in a different way and it's so easy to get overwhelmed. I found it really stressful at times, but I got through it.

Here are some ideas based on the things that I found worked really well for me when my kids were that age:

⊘ **TIDY THE PLACES YOU KNOW THEY'RE NOT GOING TO GET TO.** It might just be the inside of one cupboard but it's a great start and can still give you that sense of calm and organisation

Ø If there's a space where most of the toys are (or even a playroom) then **AVOID GETTING EVERYTHING OUT AT ONCE** and having to clear it all up afterwards. I was quite strict with getting just one or two things out and then putting them away before getting anything else out – just for my sanity. Of course, it doesn't always work, especially if there are lots of kids playing together, but it doesn't hurt to get them into the use/put-away routine from a young age.

Ø **MAKE SURE EVERYTHING HAS ITS PLACE.** Whether it's a toy box or baskets or shelves or cupboards or drawers. If there's a system it makes it easier to find things in the first place and then to organise them afterwards. That way, when I am tidying up I don't feel stressed that everything is going in one big jumble pile. Just shoving everything back in a cupboard and wedging the doors shut might provide a short-term solution, but the minute you want to get anything out and the whole lot ends up back on the floor (or on your head!), that's when it gets really overwhelming. Remember, toddlers are tornadoes. Walking, talking tornadoes, so having that organisation helps create calm for you and for them.

Ⓥ **KEEP IT SIMPLE.** You don't need expensive units or furniture. Find what works for you. It can be as simple as having, say, four baskets. If you know what goes in which basket, then at the end of the day when you're tired and just want to sit down and relax, you know what goes where and it makes it all quicker and easier. You can say to yourself, *I've just got to get the toys in those four baskets, then I'm done.* Feels good. And it also means that when they want to play with something you know where it is and don't have to turn all the baskets out on the floor to find it.

> *Make good with what you have! Tidy it up and make it functional.*

It's also really good to find coping strategies for when things can't be as organised as you'd like them to be. Sometimes it's actually good just to walk away. Because you end up thinking *I've tried so hard today and look at what I'm left with*. You overwhelm yourself and end up not sleeping properly, not eating properly, you really end up stretching yourself too thin. So in those circumstances the best thing you can do is shut the door and walk away. Take a moment for *you*. Sit down, have a cup of tea, watch a movie, do whatever you need to do. Then you'll feel fresher and much more able to tackle the task.

Again that's a principle that works in all different areas of life. And it's why at the HQ we have a little staff area where people can go just to take that bit of time out. It's really important to be able to do that in any situation, whether it's at home or work or with friends. It's just about recognising it, being able to say, *You know, I'm feeling inundated, I'm going to go to the pub, sit down and have a portion of chips and take that bit of time for me.*

NOT ENOUGH HOURS IN THE DAY

I've always been a working parent. I've done nursing full time and combined that with family life, working shifts and having various small businesses on the side. I think that's best described as pretty full on! But I've always been a busy person and I actually don't love being in a situation where I have nothing to do. I remember even as an 18-year-old, Lee's mum would say to me, 'You never sit still! Why don't you just sit and watch a movie?' While that's perfect for lots of people, for me I'm not sure that's a good thing for my brain space because I tend to use the time to overthink things and that's when I get worse with my anxiety. A lot of people message me and say they're worried that I'm going to burn out if I don't stop, but actually for me it keeps me going and really, all the things I do are one big, giant, massive coping mechanism. And keeping busy works as a big distraction from any thoughts that could creep from the back to the front again. I do truly believe that.

All the same, these days I'm running The Label Lady which is a (very) full-time job, while also still doing some nursing bank shifts and, of course, looking after three kids. So effectively I'm trying to be a full-time businesswoman and a full-time mum and clearly there are nowhere near enough hours in the day for that. So how do you make that work? This is something else people ask me all the time. And my honest, honest opinion? It doesn't always work. Sometimes it does work, but sometimes it just doesn't.

You can only do what you can do. But I do have a few ways of giving it my best shot.

⊘ **I TRY MY UTMOST TO MAKE STRICT RULES AND STICK TO THEM.** For example, my daughters ice-skate on a Monday. And I make sure that unless I'm really in dire straits at the HQ that I'm out of there by half two, I pick them up and I watch them skate. I try to be really strict about that; I say to myself *No, you work far too many hours and there is all this other stuff going on and actually it's something so important, to be there with them, to watch, to be present*, and I make it my priority

⊘ It's so easy to think I'll just do an extra hour here or I'll just do a couple of things there and suddenly you find you're working every evening and all weekend. I was really bad at this at one point. So over the last six months or so I've tried really hard to **CARVE OUT PROPER FAMILY TIME** and make sure I have one day where we're all at home together. It got to the point where we were taking the kids to the HQ and here and there and they were like, 'Can we just stay at home?' They didn't want to go out, they didn't want to go to the zoo, or the office or anywhere else, they just wanted to be at home with us.

☑ Of course it's not always possible to completely separate work and home, especially when you have your own business (more on this in chapter six). But there are ways to make it work for you as a family. The kids spend a lot of time at the HQ but I make sure they bring stuff from home so it feels more familiar. I also talk to them about it and **EXPLAIN THAT THIS IS LIFE**, lots of parents have to work, not all of them, but I do have to work and it's not negotiable. I think it's really important that they understand. And yes, some people might say, 'Well just go and get a job which is nine to five.' But selfishly, I know I wouldn't have been satisfied with that for myself. And what I do has big benefits for the family too. Lee and I work together, which is great for the kids in that we do get to do things because we have that flexibility where we don't have to change shifts or book time off to fit in with other people. I make sure I attend their school plays, I make sure that I go to their sports days. So yes, there are sacrifices but there is also privilege in being able to do those things that many other parents can't.

⊘ The truth is that it doesn't always work but we try to **FIND WAYS THAT MAKE THE BEST OF IT FOR EVERYONE**. School holidays are a nightmare for any working parent; you get four or five weeks' holiday a year and yet the schools are off for thirteen or fourteen weeks or more. It's a bit like trying to fit a pint in a shot glass. There was a time in the summer holidays when my kids ended up staying for almost two weeks straight at my sister's house. They were there the whole fortnight and she looked after them for me while I stayed here and worked because that was what needed to be done at that period of time. Does that mean I neglect my kids? No! They had the best summer ever! They were with family who love them, they had cousins to play with, my sister has an outdoor swimming pool that they spent their whole time jumping in and out of every single day. It was like they were on holiday and sometimes we just have to do these things. That's life. I paid for a childminder for two and a half, maybe three years and I have no idea how we afforded that with three kids in childcare, but you do what you need to do to make it work.

Sometimes in the school holidays I've felt really guilty that we aren't out every day, but then I had a conversation with my sister and she reminded me, 'Jemma, did we go out every day in the school holidays? No. We were at home or at our nan's house. Taking a family of five out just once in a holiday is amazing.' I just felt bad, but she's absolutely right. It's too expensive and it's not realistic and there are plenty of things we can do for no cost at all, like dog walks through the woods, playing in the stream, going to the park, having a picnic. It made me realise the children are fine! It's just me with the worry that they're not happy.

⊘ Another thing that worked for us before we had the business, which obviously won't work for everyone, is that **LEE AND I DID SHIFTS** so one of us was always with the kids. So often I would do nights and he would do days. Not ideal for lots of reasons, but again you do what you need to do to get through. Now we work together, which helps, and I'm so grateful that he was prepared to give up what he had to support me. I've seen it with many others working in small – and bigger – businesses too. And I love that the site is a partnership as much as our family.

I think even in this day and age, a lot of people still think the man should be the provider and I really disagree with this. Lee and I are a team and work together to provide for our family – both now and before The Label Lady too. I don't think there should ever be an assumption that it has to be one person or the other. And just because I run a business doesn't mean Lee doesn't play his part. Our roles might be completely different, but I think more of him as a man than ever because he has enabled me to follow my dream.

Over the last two and a half years I've spoken to a number of people in a similar position to us, who are now working alongside their partners. One thing we have all felt is what a good thing it is for equality within a relationship. As well as working together, it can offer the flexibility, say, for both parents to be able to do the school drop-offs or pick-ups or go to school events and things like that. I think flexible working since the pandemic has also helped with this too, with more people working from home for part of the week. And that can only be a good thing all round.

COPING WITH STRESS

This is another area where I think it's really important to realise that those 'Insta-perfect' lives are not a reality. Because thinking everyone else is coping with life way better than you are will only make you more stressed and that's definitely not going to help. So, for example, people might look at my stories and reels and think I'm always (or usually!) super calm, but the truth is my life is just as hectic as anyone else's. It can be a bit like the way a duck swims serenely along the surface of the water, but underneath it's paddling furiously; just because you see me being happy on Instagram or doing something amazing on social media doesn't mean that my bedroom doesn't look like an actual pigsty or hasn't been turned upside down by three children sleeping in one bed and refusing to get up in the morning after having no sleep. Or me being exhausted because I've had Lee snoring in my ear all night. So the first thing I would say is:

☑ **FOCUS ON YOU** rather than everyone else around you. Take a look at you and your life because it's all too easy to get roped into everybody else's, which doesn't give you the space to sort yourself out.

And my second thing would be:

⊘ **REACH OUT TO OTHER PEOPLE** for advice or help when you need it. There's no shame in it and we all do it! If you need something and you've got people around you, then ask, because most of the time people will say yes. Sometimes it can be quite daunting to say, 'I'm really stuck right now, would you mind grabbing so and so when you do the school run later?' Or 'On your way home could you pick me up a loaf of bread or a pint of milk?' But the majority of the time people will just say 'Of course, no worries at all'. And a small thing can be a huge weight off your shoulders. So asking people can be super helpful. When I had Hudson, Lee was working full-time, as were both my parents and siblings, and Lee's mum wasn't close by. I couldn't get Darcy to school as I couldn't drive after the Caesarean and you can't walk there from where we live due to the country lanes. So I had to ask a school mum to help, and she did. I felt so embarrassed to ask and built it all up in my head, but guess what? She couldn't have been more kind.

There will be points in your life when you'll be the one to give help and points when you'll be the one to need it – remember this; it can make you feel better for asking or saying yes when people offer. If you've just had a baby, for example, friends and family helping out with things like shopping, cooking and school runs can be the best gift of all. Make a list of what you need (lists coming into their own again!) so when people ask if there's anything you need, you have the answers to hand.

MUM GUILT

On the physical side I think I cope pretty well. I sometimes get to a point where I am very tired and I have to say to Lee, 'I need to sleep'. But a busy life can also be emotionally draining. It's emotionally draining when I think I'm not spending enough time with my children or I'm not doing enough things for them. And that holds a tremendous amount of guilt too. But at the same time, as I mentioned earlier, I do talk to the kids about it. I say to them 'If you want the nice things in life – you want to go on holiday or out with your friends or go on Christmas outings – you need to realise all these things are massive privileges and there has to be a compromise. And this is our compromise'. And I also say to them, 'Look, you can join us and be a part of all this or you can moan about it. But moaning isn't going to do anything and it's not going to change anything.'

There are certain things I always try to make sure that I do. I take the girls skating. I make sure they read every night. With Huds, if we don't read we will play phonics games or something like that. So I try not to feel guilty in that sense. I will go to assemblies and nativity plays and so on; Lee and I try to ensure we attend all their school events. And I do that mostly for them, but also to make sure I don't feel like I'm missing out on everything because you know that one day you'll blink and suddenly they're adults.

But don't feel bad if you aren't the parent who is able to read every day or help them complete every piece of homework. You are doing your best, and that's all that matters. I'm not great with homework, but we are lucky in the sense that at our kids' school, homework is optional. My thoughts are that they are already in school six hours a day, they are good children and when they get home I just want them to be able to rest and chill out without me feeling like a sergeant major. I am sure that when they go to secondary school it will change, but for now they are okay. They're learning lots, they are excellent pupils and I don't feel guilty. I'm very honest with the school, and if the children ever need extra help, I will, of course, be there.

FINDING A SENSE OF CALM

I find that I can only be calm when I feel good – and if I'm really tired and overworked I don't feel great. So what I'll do quite often is make an effort to find five minutes for me. A short break can have a huge effect and even a little bit of time out can give you the motivation to move on to the next thing. So often my calm is finding those few minutes on my own to just switch off, regroup and then I can switch back on again. I also like to do things that will give me satisfaction (again, feeling good = calm). I don't want to see my house messy so I will go and tidy up. I will restock things because I find it rewarding. I don't want to see that the inside of a cupboard is all over the place so I will go and organise it – because when I do it I can close that cupboard and breathe out a sigh of *Ahhhh, that's done*. And honestly, it might not sound like much, but even five minutes out can still feel like hours to your brain, so it's always worth making the time and space to do this. *Stop. Breathe out. Cool down.* And then you're ready to start again. It's like a reset button!

(Oh, and I should add it doesn't matter where you do it. It could be a quick walk round the block, finding a quiet spot or even sitting on the toilet – this is what Lee does. We don't have any doors on our bathrooms but we've got one loo with a lock; he put that lock in and I know that's because it's where he goes to chill. Then he comes out ready to start again. He's going to love me telling you this!)

CHAPTER FOUR

Making Your Space Work for YOU

I've already talked about the positive impact lists can make, as well as navigating the juggle of home, work and family life. But making sure that the space around you is working with you rather than against you can make an enormous difference too.

Of course, it's all too easy to believe in the myth that everyone you know is more organised than you are. I can guarantee that's not the case. Yes, I might sometimes show my house looking all clean and tidy, but it is never going to be like that 24/7 and like everyone else I have to work to make it that way, which is why often I'll also show it not looking organised at all.

I look at influencers with these super clean houses and I think, *That's amazing. How???* But I think while you can appreciate the aesthetic, these reels, posts and stories can also leave you feeling like you can't ever achieve that yourself, especially if you're like me and your kids are tornadoes running around all over the place. You just think *My house is never going to be like that* and end up putting unrealistic pressure on yourself too. And not only will that stress you out, but it can also stop you doing things; for example, you might want to have friends over but feel you don't want people to see your place because it doesn't match up to these 'ideals'. So my advice to anyone feeling this way has always been:

⊘ **DO THINGS LITTLE AND OFTEN.** We can't all have these amazing washing piles where you click and they magically disappear. We can't all have houses that are spotlessly clean and tidy from top to bottom. But getting bits done where you can really does make a difference. I'm thinking of times when Lee and I have come in and had an hour between the school run and leaving for the girls' skating so he'd be like, 'I'll do downstairs and you do upstairs and we'll just whizz all the washing together and make all the beds.' And it sounds so silly but just making the beds and whizzing the washing up and down the stairs means that when we come in at nine o'clock at night we feel a sense of order and calm.

⊘ **LOOK AT YOUR FRIENDS AND THE PEOPLE AROUND YOU,** people who aren't posting interior shots on Instagram or social media or showing off all that stuff, because the likelihood is that they will be in exactly the same boat as you. Then you realise it's quite normal. Sometimes it's easy to forget that not everything happens at the click of an Instagram finger, and you can get lost in a bubble thinking you're not doing things quickly enough. In the real world where we are all short of time, it's important to remember that even small steps can make a big difference and as long as you get everything you want to do done, it really doesn't matter how long it takes.

⊘ **USE YOUR TIME FOR YOU.** So if you've got a few minutes you might think, *You know what would make me really happy right now? If the ironing was all put away rather than sitting in the middle of the kitchen.* So do it. Don't not do it because you feel bad you're not doing something else. If that's what will make you happy, go do that, and keep your own calm while making a difference to the environment around you.

⊘ IF YOU HAVE CHILDREN, GET THEM TO HELP!

It all adds up. It doesn't matter how old they are; you're teaching them to respect things, love things, look after things, all of that. And putting their shoes on the shoe rack is not a job. It should just be an action. So when you walk in and they've chucked their shoes all over the floor and you're left to clear up the hallway, never feel guilty about calling them back to do something about it – 'Oi, before you run off, come here and put your shoes away properly.' Then that becomes a habit for them and it saves you time as you don't have to run around after them and tidy them all away. By the way, before you start thinking that my children are absolute angels, I should probably stress that this is definitely not the case and I don't always get the chance to practise what I preach. I'm thinking of the time I turned up at school in my oversized avocado Oodie and slippers, apologising for being so late because Mila was driving me crazy. The head teacher said, 'Anything in particular?' I was like 'No, I just can't deal with this'. It happens to us all!

FINDING SERENITY THROUGH SORTING!

I've talked about finding a sense of calm from taking five minutes out to reset, and from using lists to get everything cluttering up your brain out onto paper and creating a purposeful sense of order. For me another guaranteed way to feel on top of things, to have that sense of inner peace – even if it's brief! – is through organisation.

Something that the pandemic perhaps brought home to us more than ever is that whether we like it or not, there is so much in life that is completely outside of our control. For those of us who like to be in control of things, that's not the easiest thing to process.

To say it's been a turbulent couple of years is something of an understatement. From lockdowns and Brexit to strikes and political upheaval, to name just a few, all of which have impacted so many of us personally and professionally and caused huge amounts of turmoil and stress. But what have we been able to do about any of it? For the most part, absolutely nothing. And that can bring a lot of additional strain to cope with.

It might sound crazy that cleaning out a cupboard can make a difference in this situation, but I promise you, it can help. How? Because it's something you *can* exert control over. It's something you can directly influence for positive change. It's something that can restore order where before there was none. And in all those things there is calm to be found.

I believe that having control of something – even if it's something small – is so important, because it's almost that touchdown with reality. Like, I am here, I am in control of this, I am able to do something. And it starts off that thought process of positivity rather than negativity. So I think that no matter what you're like in life, whether you're an organised person or not, just doing something works because *you* did it, *you've* completed it, *you've* done it in the way that works best for your environment, your brain and that's *your* piece of control.

I look at it like this: there will always be so many factors in the world around you that you can't control, but in your home there will always be things that you can. And they're the things you're going to look at every day, you're going to be around every day. So those small steps will create a domino effect and create that calm without even thinking about it, and the next time you walk into that space you will no longer feel that sense of stress or dread.

Of course, for most of us it's always going to be an uphill battle to keep on top of everything all the time, but prioritising the areas that you use regularly can save (a lot of) time and stress. So for example, if you make packed lunches every day, have that section of the kitchen organised, because it's something that's going to keep getting used and used and used. It's all too easy to end up with 59 million Tupperware pots because you can't find what you need when you need it or the lids have gone missing or they've left that one at school or you don't know where this one is or what cupboard that one's in or you think you broke one ... so you buy more! And the pile grows and the problem gets worse and everything spirals.

I find it is quite stressful having to do lunches anyway, so if you organise that area and that part of your day it speeds things up as well as creating calm. And if you feel calm before you've even walked out of the door then that starts your day off on the right foot.

Perhaps you wear makeup and that's a part of your daily routine. But if you've got a bit of it in the bedroom and a bit of it in the bathroom, some in your handbag and a bit more here, there or all over the place, not only will it create mess and disorder but it will also mean you're spending half your time trying to find stuff before you even start. However, if you've got one station with a set of organised drawers and/or little pots where everything goes and you know that that section is eyes, that one's face, lips or maybe everyday makeup, glam/going-out stuff, etc. then there's no stress, because everything's there. It's ready to use. Job done.

Sometimes we don't have the prettiest cupboards or spaces in our homes. Social media can make us feel like this isn't normal! It is, we all have them, it's what we do with them that is important.

START SMALL

Don't think about blitzing the entire house in one go. Prioritise the areas you use the most (or that are stressing you out because they're all over the place). Even organising just one thing is a great start. Depending on the size of the room or area, it might take a bit of time to do but it will save much more time in the long run, as well as creating order and satisfaction. What's not to love?

One of the best spaces I've organised is my son's wardrobe and it's made such a difference. Hudson loves it so much. My girls loved knowing where everything was in their cupboards and he really does too. He goes in and gets himself an outfit and it's such a nice feeling. And I love that here organisation is not only about order but also helping to create independence.

The cupboard was in a bit of a state when we started. But no more! Here's my step by step guide to how I sorted it out.

1. The cupboard (an IKEA Pax double wardrobe – lots of people have asked!) has a hanging rail at the top, so things like tops, shirts and jackets, etc. were all hung neatly there. Arrange them by short sleeve, long sleeve, by season, by occasion – whatever is going to work best (and make things easiest) for you.

2. In the bottom of the cupboard we fitted a set of drawers and clearly labelled each one. For example, we have one for pants and socks, one for shorts and swimwear, another for pyjamas and so on. There's a smaller basket drawer at the bottom labelled 'bits and bobs' so even those things have their place.

3. Where needed, within the drawers I added smaller baskets to divide them. For example, one basket for pants and one for socks helps to stop them ending up in one big messy tangle.

4. On the right-hand side we fitted another drawer for trousers and shelves, with labelled baskets, for things such as wipes. And we added a pull-out basket for shoes at the top.

5. As Huds is still learning to read – he knows letters and phonics but I wanted to make it easy for him until he can read properly – I then added picture labels so he can see at a glance what's in each drawer. These (from The Label Lady, naturally!) make everything so clear for him and are perfect for using in younger children's rooms.

6. I've always been a big fan of using baskets in drawers to give everything its place and keep things perfectly organised. Not just in bedrooms; they're ideal in kitchens, bathrooms and offices too. They work really well if the things take up similar amounts of space. I really love drawer inserts too as they're so flexible and you can make each space as big or as small as you like. I find I'm using them more and more, and though I say so myself, my girls' dressing-table drawer is a work of art! Brushes, bows, clips – all ordered and beautiful. Total satisfaction. You don't need to spend a fortune on matchy-matchy baskets and tubs by the way. Shallow boxes can do the job perfectly. I've used the ones from my GHDs and from toiletry gift sets or fancy chocolates and so on – the ones made of really thick card are perfect for this. So many household things can be repurposed when it comes to organisation. The cardboard tube from inside a kitchen roll? Thread your hair ties and scrunchies over it. Not only does it keep them tidy – and these things have a habit of getting *everywhere* – but you can also see what you need at a glance. And it's free too! Win win win.

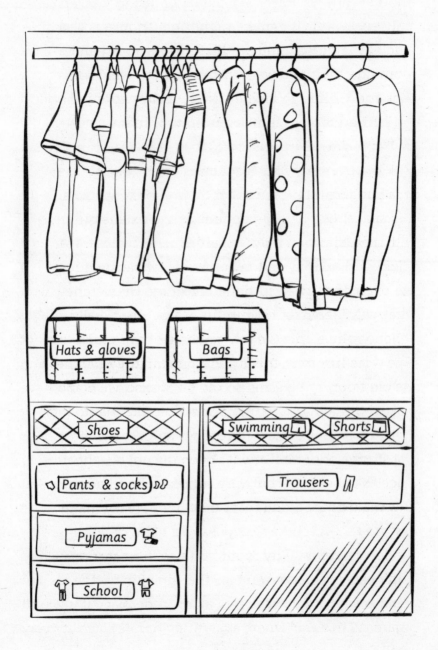

Another thing that was very satisfying to sort out was my 'ugly cupboard'. When we bought our house it was quite higgledy-piggledy and we had a front room and a back room and then this weird inner hallway which led to the back room and the kitchen. It was really strange. And in the kitchen there was an oven, literally in the centre of the house, built into the wall. When we did our extension we took the oven out and redid everything else, but we were on a budget and there was a limit to what we could do with this space. Lee did 90 per cent of the extension himself, with help from family including his brother (who's a bricklayer) and my dad. When we'd finished and removed the oven and knocked out a chimney, we were left with what was literally a hole in the wall. And it really is ugly – hence the name, which seems to have stuck. It's got pipe work in it from the original build in the Seventies and the old flooring tiles and so on. Of course, we could have plastered it and put in lights and stuff like that to make it pretty but we just didn't have the budget at the time so we just stuck a door on it and it's been the ugly cupboard ever since! Not beautiful but very functional and a space that now makes sense, and that's the bit that really matters.

We don't have a utility room, so I use it for storing all that stuff that you don't want in the kitchen cupboards but could easily end up scattered all over the place if it wasn't organised in a way where everything has its place. It's very small but Lee put shelves in made from stuff left over from building the extension and we gave it a coat of paint and added jars, labels and hooks, so now it's a really practical space. It houses what we need it to house and gets things out of the way, but still in a place where everything is easily accessible.

I didn't do it all at once – partly because I needed to give the paint time to dry, partly because I needed to have a wash before turning up to school covered in streaks of white emulsion, but mainly because it's good to build in breaks to restore calm.

This is how I organised the space.

1. I added layered shelves. At the top I have baskets with loop tags for things like wax melts and small tools such as screwdrivers, for when you want to put batteries in a toy and don't want to have to go and root around in the garage to find what you need. Those sorts of small household items all go up there.

2. The next layer is dogs – dog food, dog treats and so on. We have two dogs and they need slightly different things so it really helps to have everything organised in this way.

3. Below that is all the hoover parts – the attachments you can stick on (I never know what they're technically called so let's go with the curly bit, the straight bit and so on!) and then the iron sits next to those.

4. Clipped on to the wall I have a long dustpan and brush. Also the hoover – it's a cordless one and it needs plugging in to charge, so Lee drilled through the wall so we could have a plug socket in there, and an extension lead so we can charge the handheld vacuum in there too.

5. On the floor underneath I have the huge bag of dog food with a scooper, the clothes airer and my mop and bucket. And there's room at the back for bulk cleaning products which don't fit in a regular cupboard, so I can keep them out of the way after I've decanted them into the bottles we use on a daily basis.

Everything we need is in that tiny – but tidy – space. It's very compact but it works!

KEEPING TOYS UNDER CONTROL

I recently did a big reorganisation of our playroom. This used to be part of our garage, which ran the whole length of our house, and by repurposing half of it we created a new room, which has been a much better use of the space for our family. There is still some garage left to keep tools and garden bits, but the rest became a playroom and a downstairs loo. One of my friends from college came over and hand-painted incredible murals and I love it so much that if we ever move I think I will have to get the new owners to sign something to say they will never paint over it! In a house with very little storage, having somewhere to put all the kids' stuff has been a game changer, but the principles of organising it all are the same, whether you have a separate room or a space in a living room or a cupboard where you keep everything. The thing with children's toys is that they seem to multiply when you turn your back. Christmas and birthdays generally mean more stuff and that in turn means finding somewhere to put it all.

I've found that replacing rather than adding is the best way forward and stops it all getting completely overwhelming. We go through what's already there and find things that they've either got too old for or lost interest in and they understand that being able to say goodbye to those makes room for the new things. Those goodbyes are not always easy – letting things go can be really hard. If it's something that's been super special to them that I think their children will play with – in the same way my own kids have played with my Polly Pockets – then I will store them away, but otherwise I like to see toys get used and that means they aren't always going to be with my children for ever. The good thing is that toys have great long-term value. My kids' pre-school loves getting pre-loved toys and after-school clubs and playgroups are often really grateful to get toys in good condition. When my children have outgrown things, it makes so much sense to allow others to enjoy them.

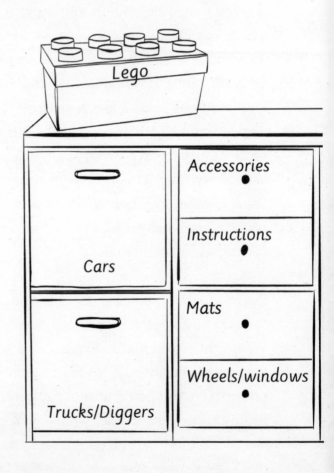

Now the children are older, a lot of their stuff can go in their bedrooms, but for things that they enjoy doing together and which require a bit more space, having the playroom is still really useful. Lego is the perfect example and I've found a bit of organisation has really helped the children to make the most of it. I did a huge blitz recently because I wanted them to have the space to build and show off their creations and to be able to find all the bits without having to sort through a massive jumble of pieces.

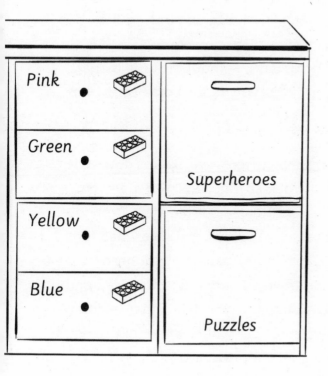

I used IKEA Kallax units and in the drawers I added inserts – labelled of course! – for various colours and parts such as doors, windows, figures and so on. If you don't have space for this, then stacked and labelled tubs will do the job brilliantly too.

By putting the Kallax units lengthways rather than upright it meant that everything was within easy reach and we kept the top clear so they could use it to show off their creations. We also made a rule that once the top was full they'd have to break down something to replace it with another.

They love using their imaginations to build things and I love watching them create. And by organising it all we have made a space where they can come together to play and build happily for days, without creating carnage elsewhere. Anyone who has ever stepped on a Lego brick will recognise the value of this!

I love it when my kids are being creative, but the downside can be that it seems to involve so much STUFF. Paints, pens, glue, stickers, glitter – and that's just the start. Working out where to put it all so it's a) easily accessible when they want it and b) still neat and tidy can be a real headache. My answer? A crafting trolley! Everything organised and labelled. It can be wheeled to the table when they're doing stuff and can be easily stored elsewhere when they're not. Perfect. I'd have loved one of these as a kid SO much!

You can get trolleys pretty cheaply from various retailers such as IKEA, Hobbycraft and many more. They are great for all sorts of things, but this is how we've made the best use of ours:

1. Firstly, I used brightly coloured labels to decorate the trolley. This has two advantages. Firstly, it makes it looks so appealing to the children – and I'd far rather they were enjoying themselves with the things they have in it than asking for screens all the time. Secondly, the labels also have a practical purpose. Everything has its assigned place and no one has to ask me what goes where. This also means that when they're done, tidy-up time is quick and easy rather than stuff being thrown in any which way (and which then means having to sort it all out again another time.)

2. The trolley has three levels and I've arranged everything around size and type and for ease of access. On the top level, we have pencils, crayons, markers and pens. These are stored in pots (one for each category). You can find cheap pots that are perfect for this all over the place; as ever, practicality is the most important thing. I wanted pots that were sturdy but also looked good. Either way, there's no more scrabbling around for a pencil hidden under a pile of other things.

3. I found it easier to label the *outside* of the trolley with generic things such as 'arts and crafts', 'pens and pencils' etc. That way if the things in the pots change, the new ones will still have a defined place to go.

4. The middle shelf. I found a pack of ten brightly coloured baskets which were the perfect size, so lined up five of those to store various things like Play-Doh, stamps, ink, slime and glitter, etc. (The rest of the baskets I used elsewhere – nothing wasted!)

5. The bottom level is the perfect place for bottles of paint, along with brushes. I also found some pots with lids to keep stick-on shapes, pom poms, stickers, beads, sequins, pipe cleaners and so on – again this stops all these things ending up in one big heap which no one can be bothered to sift through. The pots are also much more practical than keeping things in their original packets, which have a habit of spilling or splitting.

6. Need more space? You can also get pots to clip onto the trolley and I've used them on the ends of the top and middle shelves. They're perfect for tissue paper and scissors as well as various other bits and bobs. Again, everything has its place!

7. Most of our art supplies were given as Christmas and birthday presents. They often come in large sets, so I decant things for the trolley, and then refill when needed. The rest can be stored out of the way in a cupboard; the kids already have everything they need in the trolley, so have no need to access it.

I've applied much the same principle to the drawers my girls have in their bedrooms. These drawers contain things they use every day, so the stationery they need for homework and all the stuff for getting ready – pens, pencils, hair ties, hair brushes and so on – so they have their own clearly labelled spaces. If they see this sort of organisation in front of them every day, it becomes part of them, that's their visual every morning. It also helps with routine, because then whenever someone says, 'Where's your brush?', they know where it is. I got so fed up of saying, 'Where's your this or that?' only to be met with, 'I don't know.' I'm sure many other parents will be all-too-familiar with that scenario! It's a bit like when they take their shoes off in the car and then they're like, 'I don't know where my shoes are.' I'm like, 'I watched you take them off in the car.' Why is that a thing? I have no idea.

So the girls' drawers are labelled beauty, hair, stationery, craft and so on. Darcy also has one for snacks; I've never let them eat upstairs, like never, ever, ever, but I've had to remind myself that she is ten years old, and they're going to be teenagers who are going to eat in their rooms whatever I say. And, actually, it's not a bad thing to give her a new sense of responsibility. So I've said to her, 'Look, the deal is that if you do have snacks up there' – like if she's been to the shops and got a stash of sweets or whatever – if you're not eating it, it goes in the snack drawer. I don't want to see it, ever.' So anything that's opened or half eaten has to go away, out of sight. I don't want sweet papers and wrappers and half-empty bottles all over the place. So far it's working really well. I'm trying to instill these sorts of things now, and hopefully they'll stay with them. (That said, I did make her go out and buy herself a bin and take responsibility for dealing with it after I discovered she had been putting all the rubbish back in the drawer! No more complaints about banana skins being smelly. Put it in the bin and empty it as needed!)

Label the drawers. This means the space is set and encourages you not to fill it with random items that won't get used.

I used simple-to-read labels, so that the girls can easily see what goes in each place.

Drawers around a desk mean you have extra storage, so leave the bulk of the desk space clear. This is important to make sure the desk can be used at all times.

Both girls love hair and make-up so we made sections for this, as well as practical sections for their homework and crafts.

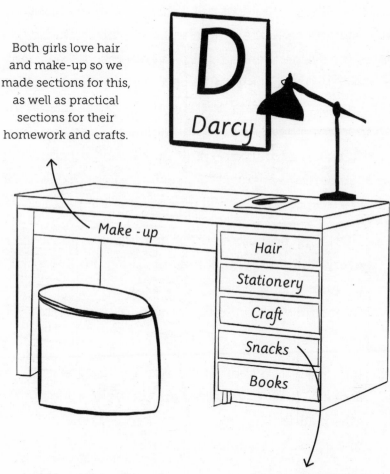

Organise the drawers into sections to give items a home. Using boxes keeps items separated, meaning they are easy to find and use.

MAKING YOUR FRIDGE WORK FOR YOU

Back in the kitchen, one more great area to work on is your fridge. It's something we all use multiple times a day, day in, day out, yet do we make it work how we really need it to? The evidence suggests not. When I asked my followers on Instagram whether their fridges were organised, a whopping 78 per cent said no. Even more (88 per cent) admitted that food regularly gets wasted. There are so many reasons why that's an issue, not least because of the fact food costs have risen so much recently and you don't want to spend a fortune on stuff only to end up chucking it out. So here are my tips to make finding out of date food behind a load of bottles and jars a thing of the past.

1. DON'T get home from the shops, rush to unpack everything and chuck it all in so it's put away as quickly as you can. That's a guaranteed way to ensure you will end up not knowing where anything is.

2. Before you go shopping (or your online shop arrives), take everything out of your fridge, check all the use by or best before dates and give the fridge a quick once over.

3. I like to use fridge mats – I'm a big fan. You can find them in most homeware stores and they are anti-slip and great for holding spills. You can cut them to size to protect your shelves.

4. If you're organising your fridge for the first time, plan your layout before putting any food away. It makes it much easier to see what works and play around with it until you're happy with it.

5. Labelled fridge trays and tubs are great to make the most of your space. Tubs are great for stacking to optimise shelf space but you can still see instantly what's where. Move things around so that the things you use the most are more accessible and it all works for you. For example, in my fridge I have a section quite low down for cut up fruit so when the kids ask I can just go in and grab it. I keep treats near the top of the fridge so little hands can't reach.

6. At the top I like to use a Lazy Susan for all my condiments and jars. Not only do I quite enjoy the spinning (!), but it also means it's easy to see what you have and nothing gets lost because it's been shoved to the back. Easy access is key.

7. In the drawers I like to put my salad and veg into containers rather than just bundling bags of stuff in and hoping for the best. It makes it far easier to see what's in there and it helps with the moisture that makes things go off faster. In fact some fridge manufacturers actually recommend you remove all the packaging to avoid that condensation.

Take items out of packaging where possible, especially in the drawers. This saves the irritation of someone leaving an empty packet in the fridge!

If you have little ones that eat as fast as mine, you can prep fruit and snacks by cutting up portions and putting them in easy to reach places in the fridge.

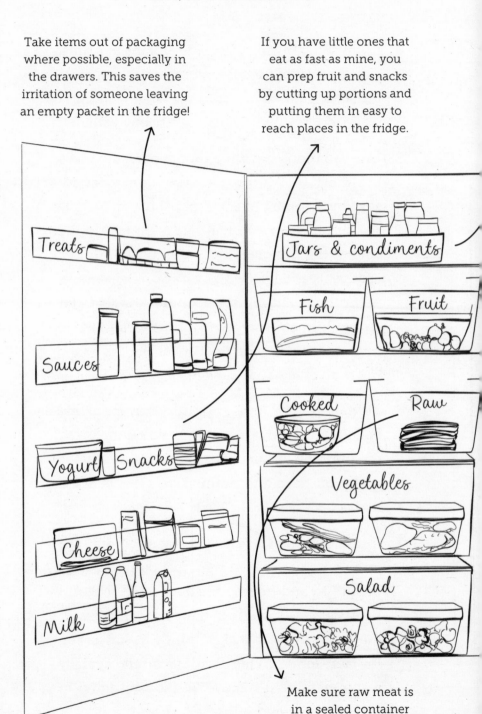

Make sure raw meat is in a sealed container that cannot leak.

Split the fridge into sections with labels to ensure the items return to these places each time you refill.

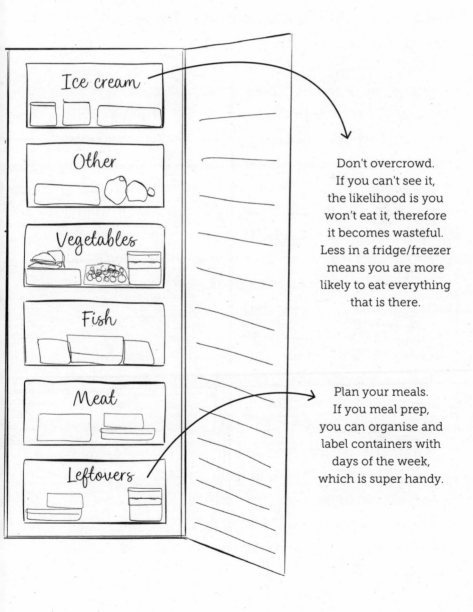

Don't overcrowd. If you can't see it, the likelihood is you won't eat it, therefore it becomes wasteful. Less in a fridge/freezer means you are more likely to eat everything that is there.

Plan your meals. If you meal prep, you can organise and label containers with days of the week, which is super handy.

I had so many great reactions when I showed how to do this in my stories. So don't just take my word for it that it works. As one follower wrote when they tried it, 'Honestly, I'm such a normal person but I've now started to change the way I do things and seen how small changes can truly make such a big difference.'

As with all these things, it's all about making it work for YOU according to your own needs and priorities. One thing that is always important to me is the lines. I'm a total perfectionist so I'm really bad with eye levels – things need to be straight! Poor Lee, he can't even hang a photo frame without me being like 'No, it's wonky'. I'm the same when I put my jars in the cupboards. If the labels aren't straight it's not happening! My sister won't even apply her own labels now – she even said it on Instagram – because she knows I will see them!

That's my own little foible, though, and precision is really not the most important thing. Remember, it doesn't have to be pretty – it has to be functional, and that's what matters most. Functional will always be more important than immaculate. Labelling things and knowing where everything is means it's doing what it needs to do. If you haven't got ten of the same pots or your tubs and baskets don't match, it really doesn't matter in the slightest, as long as the organisational side means that it works for you, your home or your family.

HOW TO DECLUTTER WITHOUT
GOING THE FULL MARIE KONDO

It doesn't have to be all or nothing! And again, I think this is another area where it's good to start small ... trying to do the whole house in one go will just be overwhelming. So I might take one drawer and rather than just trying to make a pile of things to throw away and a pile of things to keep, I will organise it instead.

One important thing to remember is that decluttering doesn't necessarily mean chucking things out. In a way it's a bit like a version of the brain unscramble on page 40 – but instead of getting everything out in your head and organising it in a list, you're sorting through your things and making them more accessible so the space (drawer/cupboard, etc.) is functional. And that's the key.

You might find that you are able to arrange everything in a better way so you can actually make use of it. After all, if it's all in a big, messy heap, how do you even know what's in there? You might find that everything is worth keeping or there might be loads of stuff that you don't even need; sometimes it can be a mystery as to why or how it ended up in the drawer in the first place and that's a total waste. So that's why you start by reorganising. You can see what you do and don't use and *then* you can make sensible decisions about what to keep or get rid of. It's the same principle as the brain unscramble. Get everything out in front of you, see what you've got and work out what to do with it. That mascara has sat there for four months and never been touched. Why are you keeping it? That pen doesn't even work – straight in the bin. What you have to ask yourself is, what use is it to you or what value does it add to your life?

CHAPTER
FIVE

Living with Anxiety

 | |

When I was younger I was very happy-go-lucky, and I never really had a care in the world. I lived for the moment – going on holidays, hanging out with my friends, having a good time. I met Lee when I was 18; I went clubbing with the girls, he was one of their boyfriends' friends. We talked all night and he kept offering to buy me drinks (to which my response was that I could buy my own drinks, thank you, I didn't need a man to do it!) Anyway, by the end of the night it was fair to say we'd both had a few.

A couple of days later he messaged and asked if I'd like to go out. I said I didn't see the point because I didn't think he'd remember what I looked like, who I was, but he said of course he would! So he arranged to pick me up and came to the house and I said to my sister, 'Go get in the car.' She was like, 'What?', I said, 'Go get in the car, that boy thinks he remembers me and wants to take me out, so let's see if he really does'. So she got in the car and he drove off with her because he didn't notice! Let's say he was not impressed with my test to see if he did actually remember me!

Obviously 18 was quite young to be in a relationship and stay in a relationship for all these years, but he had no problems with me going out a lot and going away with my friends, which I did every year. In fact he empowered me to do that, wanted me to be as free as I wanted to be and that kept me so secure in the relationship at such a young age because I was never held back by him. He's been incredibly supportive from the very start and I'm so glad that he got to know me before the anxiety. In those days, I was the life and soul of any party and always up for a laugh, although I was also pretty sensible too, and knew where the line was. I worked hard, played hard and loved my carefree life. I had absolutely no idea how quickly that was all going to change.

Having my first baby knocked me for six. I was thrilled to be pregnant but hadn't factored in the horrific morning sickness that I suffered with Darcy. Lee had booked a holiday to Egypt that we couldn't change and I thought I'd be fine. I was nine weeks and really tired so I ended up spending most of the holiday sleeping. But I was SO sick – to the point that my poo went white! I tried so hard to get out and explore. We went on a trip to Luxor and had to fly there. Lee literally had to give me a piggyback everywhere because I felt so sick, but I didn't want to miss out and felt so bad for him. He was so good. I called my midwife and said, 'I can't eat, I can't drink, I don't know what to do.' I remember exactly what he said: 'Get yourself to McDonalds every day and drink a large milkshake'. I cried. I was like, 'I'm not allowed milkshake' and he just said, 'You need it', I guess knowing that it was from a safe place and would give me the fat and sugar I was lacking and it was that or a hospital visit! So I sipped a milkshake every night and though I tried to enjoy the holiday, I just couldn't.

The second trimester was completely different. I remember waking up one day and realising I didn't feel sick any more. It was the funniest feeling, like a light switch being flipped. I had to keep questioning myself through the day ... *Do I feel sick? No I don't.* And from that point I had no problems at all.

I was only twenty-four, which is relatively young these days, but even so, the thought of looking after a baby had never scared me at all as I was so used to dealing with children at work. I'd not long qualified as a paediatric nurse and worked all the way through my pregnancy. Other than the early sickness, I sailed through it all, totally care-free. Everything was great – until suddenly it wasn't.

TRIGGER WARNING

The following pages contain references to
themes of traumatic childbirth and post-natal
anxiety, which some individuals may
find distressing.

My due date came and went. I wasn't worried; I knew they'd let you go up to two weeks over. All good. But gradually I realised that somehow I just didn't feel quite right, so they ended up inducing me on day ten. I was still pretty calm; being a nurse, none of the hospital stuff really fazed me at all. The first stage of induction is a pessary, so they popped that in and hooked me up to a monitor and left us to it until the contractions started to kick in. Lee and I were happily playing cards, but once a nurse, always a nurse, so I also kept half an eye on the monitor too. Within minutes I noticed that the baby's heart rate kept dipping, and so I got someone to go and find our midwife. I told him that something wasn't right and the heartbeat wasn't what it should be and I remember him picking up the graph, looking down at it and then back at me. He said 'You know what's coming, don't you?' and hit the emergency buzzer and then everything happened so fast.

They had to get the baby out as quickly as possible, so as they were moving me from the pre-labour ward they were literally stripping me, pulling my clothes off in the corridor to speed things up. I was completely in shock, I have never felt anything like it. I was shaking so much that when they were trying to cannulate me and get the needle in I physically couldn't keep my arm still, they were having to hold it to stop it from shaking.

At one point they didn't even have a surgery space so they were going to have to do it in the labour room. One of the midwives came over and gave me a massive hug and told me that it would all be okay, but I was completely traumatised and in shock and struggling to accept that my baby might not make it. In these situations they usually do a general anaesthetic to get the baby out faster, but I was in such a state I begged them not to put me to sleep. In that moment I felt I had to be present for the Caesarean. My greatest fear was going to sleep and then waking up to no baby.

Fortunately we did make it into theatre, and it was all a bit of a blur as everything seemed to be happening so fast. I do remember one of the women, though, who had the monitor on my belly and was shouting, 'There's a low heart rate, there's no heart rate' – which definitely didn't help the trauma – and my midwife yelling, 'Put it down' and saying 'It makes no difference right now, we're here for Jemma and we need to be here for Jemma'. They cut me open and pulled the baby out and she screamed, but I was so full of drugs at that point I just remember saying to Lee, 'You're green. Why are you green? You look like slime.'

I remember Lee having to ring my parents before I went down for surgery and just not knowing what to say, but my family being my family, when I came out from the C-section, they were all there waiting to make sure I was OK.

When Darcy came out, the whole paediatric resuscitation team was there. She was fine though very small; my placenta had stopped working and she'd stopped growing. I was so cold after the surgery. I just lay there under what they call a bear hugger. I think the shock had kicked in, so I wasn't allowed to hold her in that moment. My dad came in and hugged me and she was just laying there. I didn't feel like I had given birth, I didn't know what I felt, but I remember he said to me, 'She's so perfect, have you held her?' I said no but told him he could; I didn't feel like I wanted to. It was the oddest feeling, but for nine months you build up to this moment you're going to have with your baby, the feelings, the pictures, the skin to skin ... but I was just like, *What the F has happened to me and is that baby even mine?* Neither Lee nor I got to hold her. She just lay in the incubator alone.

Darcy's observations in the first 24 hours were showing that she might have an infection so she was put onto intravenous antibiotics and they kept us in for a week. I had trouble feeding – in hindsight I think she had a tongue tie like my other two did after her – but I was still traumatised, and there was very little post-birth support available. At the time I didn't see it at all though, I was used to seeing kids with cancer, broken bones, breathing problems and more though my work, and here I was with a baby that was healthy and so I felt I should just get on with it, I could deal with it.

I honestly thought what I was experiencing was normal, and this was just how you felt after having a baby; I just wasn't very impressed that no one had thought to warn me. I had a lot going on at the time. We were buying a house and it all got delayed so that we completed while I was in hospital. I went in there from one place and then home to another where everything needed doing. Suddenly nothing in my life was familiar – I wasn't at work, I was living in a new place, I didn't feel I belonged. It was all very disjointed and between all that, the birth and the demands of a newborn – I think the combination became a volcano that erupted, although at the time I didn't even realise it. I just thought, well, everyone else must feel like this too, so I've just got to suck it up and get on with it.

The way I dealt with it at first was by sleeping a lot. People always say you should nap when the baby does, but newborns basically don't do anything except sleep, feed and poo, so I found myself falling down a rabbit hole where I was sleeping day and night. And although my mum kept encouraging me to get up and do things, I didn't see it as a problem. Again, I figured it was normal.

But I felt very alone. After the C-section I wasn't allowed to drive for six weeks and it felt like I'd lost my independence. Lee went back to work and it was just me at home with the baby in silence. Just silence.

The house needed decorating. In my head I thought I'd maybe go back to work a few months after the birth ... I think I was just very immature in that sense. I was only 24 and suddenly it felt like from nowhere we had a mortgage to pay and a baby to take care of ... all these things I had no experience of, and I think suddenly everything caught up with me at once. I really lost who I was and ended up not wanting to get dressed, still sleeping all the time. My mum made me realise I had to do something about it and try to find myself again. I needed to convince myself that I wasn't crazy – and that was when I started to understand what anxiety was. I knew nothing about it before. I was a real do-anything kind of person and then boom – suddenly I became someone who was consumed by a feeling of doom every single day with no understanding of why. I just didn't get it.

As soon as I could drive again, I booked one of those baby massage groups. Darcy was about six weeks old. I was still struggling to breastfeed – it felt like I just didn't get it. I tried so hard and was still doing it but not with any confidence. I turned up at the group and saw all these mums smiling and chatting and feeding. I felt even more alone. I'm sure they weren't, but it felt like they were all sitting in a circle and staring at me, like *Who's the kid with a kid? She doesn't belong here.* I hated that feeling so much that it put me off going back. I wanted to stop breastfeeding but didn't know what to do. I just felt so very lost.

I did go back to work really quickly after just three months, because I thought I was going mad and felt I couldn't just sit at home and do nothing. I remember the matron saying to me, 'You don't have to be here, your baby's so little, go home and be with her.' But I was convinced I needed to be working. I had been open about everything at my 'keeping in touch days' and in terms of the actual work there were no issues at all. But actually, it was too early. Caring for my patients wasn't ever a problem, but when it came to looking after myself, going back too soon definitely didn't help. And then the panic really set in. Panic that I was going to die, that my heart was just going to stop. I used to say to the other nurses that something wasn't right, and I used to time us all walking laps of the ward. Then I'd have to compare heartbeats to make sure mine wasn't any different from theirs. I'd be getting them to do ECGs on me and asking the doctor if I was alive and my readings were normal ... I used to do stuff like that all the time, and they would go with it because they knew I needed to in order to carry on with my day – they were so good about it. And they would try to make me laugh, make me smile to distract me.

Apart from work, though, I pretty much stopped going out; I didn't want to be in crowded or busy places. When Darcy was four months old, Lee and my mum persuaded me to go away with my friends for a few days because they wanted me to feel like me again. At the start of the trip my friends kept asking if I was OK and whether I was sure I wanted to be there, and I had to ask them to stop. I felt like I was losing myself all over again and I just needed to have a good time. And in the end I did, I really did. I had almost forgotten what that life felt like and I had the best four days, but when we got back, almost as soon as we landed, that rain cloud appeared right over my head again and all I could think was, *I've got to come back to all this again.* It absolutely wasn't that I didn't want my baby or to be a mum. I just felt like I was walking back into the fear, while the holiday had been a complete detachment from that feeling. I was scared all the time of something happening to me.

Not long after that, I reached a point where I couldn't sleep at night. I have a hearing problem, one good ear and one bad. And if I was laying on my good ear I couldn't hear the baby crying. Even if I started off one way, I would turn over in my sleep and Lee would have to wake me up. I built a fear around that as well, thinking *What if something happens to her and I don't hear?* That made it impossible to drop off.

Then I started worrying about dying in my sleep and basically sent myself over the edge – another reason not to close my eyes. I was stressed and exhausted, which made it really tough given I now had a baby daughter to care for. But it didn't stop there. I began to wake Lee in the early hours asking him to stay awake too, because otherwise if I died no one would know because it was the middle of the night ... At first he didn't really understand what was happening, how

I'd gone from the Jemma he'd always known to this. I think at first he felt it was a phase, like she will be fine now she's stopped breastfeeding or when she's had a few days away or whatever. But at that point he realised that it was a very real problem.

When it didn't get any better, he would help me find ways to cope. He'd say 'Every time you have a panic, we're going to do something', so he'd make me have a shower, or put a wash on, or empty the dishwasher or get me to help cook a meal – even if it was three o'clock in the morning, just to make sure I wasn't sitting still and to make me stop thinking about it for a bit. And he did that every single time, no matter where, no matter when.

I needed that one person who would be there at three in the morning or four in the afternoon or ten o'clock at night. Often I'd ring him and he might be at work, up on a roof, and he'd leave the phone on loudspeaker so I knew he was there; I might be washing up, not even talking, but I just needed to know he was on the other end of it. And I'm so grateful because even now, I know no matter what I am doing, he will be there for me or will come and pick me up or whatever I need, and that's how I eventually started to rebuild my own trust in myself.

But before that point it was really tough, and I think it took me a long time to realise that this really wasn't just something that everyone goes through. In the end I realised that I needed to do something about it. I did eventually see the doctor, which was an important thing to do. I told him I felt like I was going crazy and I needed some proper help. I wasn't letting it stop me do things at that point; I was looking after my baby, who I adored, I was going to work, but inside my head I wasn't happy and couldn't continue feeling that way every single day. It's obviously not healthy to wake up in fear of what your day holds, so it was absolutely time to get professional help.

But I was so scared of dying that I felt I couldn't take any medication in case that contributed to it. I didn't want to do group therapy either, so eventually they booked me in with a therapist. I used to have Darcy with me in my arms because Lee was at work. That was my hour to sit there and have someone make me feel that I was going to be okay.

I'd say, 'I just need you to tell me that I'm not going to die' and in fact she would say the opposite, that we are all going to die at some point. But she helped me work out why I was feeling the way I was. She literally listened to me spout absolute garbage for about ten months and she just sat and listened. She helped me understand that my feelings were very real but that they were also irrational and I had to learn to deal with them. And I had no choice but to listen to her because I didn't want to take the medication route, and something had to give. So that's what I did and it made a real difference.

But things changed when I was pregnant with Mila. I'd always wanted to have my children close together. There was also a part of me that thought that if I got pregnant again then maybe I could beat the anxiety because I'd remember what I did last time and almost challenge it. Thinking back, I'd already tried that in a way; I had a miscarriage at 22 and my first thought after that was, *Oh God, now I need to get pregnant again* because I wanted to have that form of control around the situation. So having a second, then a third child was in part wanting to increase my family, part wanting to change how things had been the first time, but also a bit of a distraction mechanism. In hindsight that didn't necessarily help, and in all honesty I don't think I really learned to cope with it better until about a year and a half ago, because just as I was making progress I would have another baby, and the mix of hormones and emotions didn't give me the chance to get properly better. I never had the chance to catch up with my head.

It wasn't easy. None of my friends had kids. They just thought I'd turned into crazy Jemma. I stopped drinking when I went out because I was so scared of what alcohol would do to me. And then obviously they were like, 'Why are you not drinking? Have a drink.' So I used to pretend, ask for shots of water or lemonade. If we went to a club I would feel the beat of the music and think it was going to alter my heart rhythm and then I'd have to leave. They just didn't get it; they were still 24 and partying through life. But when they started having babies of their own they understood much more.

Dealing with all this was tough but there have been other things for me too, which have definitely added to it. When I was pregnant with Hudson it was Mila's second birthday and she became very unwell with encephalitis, an infection on her brain, after a normal childhood virus which she seemed to be recovering from well (I should add that this is very rare). We were on a mountain train with my grandma and all of a sudden she started fitting uncontrollably. Being on a train we had no oxygen, we had no phone signal, but luckily there was a heart surgeon near us who offered to help and took her off me; she was blue and I was devastated thinking *What can he do for her?* The train had a walkie talkie which they used to get in touch with the main station, and they had to call an ambulance, then relay the message back up to us to let us know what was going on. They couldn't get a main ambulance to come up to us so they tried a car and said if that didn't work they'd have to walk us down to meet it. Then when we got to the hospital, she was still having constant seizures so they had to put her into an induced coma. From that point on, both Lee and I really suffered from what I believe was post-traumatic stress disorder and even though it has nothing to do with it, we developed this fear about the children choking and not being able to breathe. That stayed with us both for a long time and was a huge trigger for me; sometimes there are triggers in your life and it's not until you look back a few years later that you even realise how they've affected you.

UNDERSTANDING YOUR ANXIETY

I found that learning about what's happening and why it's happening, and through that starting to understand my anxiety, has absolutely been key to moving forwards.

I think for me a lot of this has been about control, or lack of it. I'm a very matter of fact person. I'm not very emotional. So the anxiety, the being overwhelmed by the feelings, really knocked me.

When I went to see the therapist, she pointed out that I always had to have a plan for a plan. It goes with the organisation thing – it's just the way my brain works. As a child I used to get quite angry when a plan didn't go to plan, because I was like, I have spent all this time organising this plan and making it happen. And if it didn't happen, I used to struggle with how to deal with that. It was interesting to learn about that; I remember the therapist explaining to me that that was where I needed to start unravelling things. Because otherwise you get to a point where you're like, *It didn't go according to plan, so now what?* And then panic. It's been hugely important for me to learn that you can't control everything, but you *can* find ways to cope when things don't go how you want them to. It is something I'm generally getting better at and I try really, really, really hard. But I do still struggle with it and have to talk myself out of those negative feelings.

One of the most important things is to understand when something is simply out of your control, so stressing about it isn't going to change anything. Sometimes at work I find myself in this position and have to say to myself, *I can do nothing about this. This is completely out of my hands.* So there's no point in me getting so stressed or so anxious about it that it ruins my day, my week, my month. In fact I need to let it go and accept what will be will be. When it's something outside my own area, what can I do? Take the Royal Mail strikes in the lead-up to Christmas, for example. I know it's not the postman's fault, I get it. But at the same time it was crippling small businesses.

My inbox was almost empty, it was clear, we were on top of it and everything was fine. And then suddenly it was full of literally hundreds of emails from worried people who were panicking they weren't going to get their parcels in time. That guilt on me was massive. I had to read all those emails and just repeat over and over, 'I'm sorry', 'I'm sorry', 'I'm sorry'. And at the end of the day if the orders didn't arrive I was the one who was going to lose all the time, effort and money I'd put into them – all gone. And then I'd potentially lose them as customers too. So when I looked at it from that point of view, yes, I struggled. I struggled a lot. But again I was lucky to have Lee – who we call Laid Back Lee – who was able to turn round and say 'This isn't your fault. It's completely out of your hands.' (Though he wasn't the one who had to read all those emails, so he didn't have that emotional pull which definitely made it easier for him.)

When my anxiety was at its worst, the therapist and the support of my family helped a lot, and Lee, as ever, being my safe person who really understood has definitely made a difference in getting through the most difficult times. I also threw myself into work and spent my life coming up with ideas for various businesses. But for a long time I felt like I had lost myself. It's only now Hudson is at school and my body has had some time to recover that it's finally got a lot better. I've had the chance to catch up with my head and really rationalise it all and understand that it was a feeling rather than a physical problem, and I needed to know how to handle that feeling. Because it's the fear that actually gets you.

It's not completely gone, though, and I do still have days like that. There was one very recently and once again Lee really helped me through it. He doesn't harp on about it, he distracts me from it. That night, my mum had the kids and we went to do a food shop. Not exactly anything major. We went to Argos and I bought a light bulb, and I started to get that feeling of being overwhelmed. I needed water so we went to the supermarket, got a big bottle and ran over to the bananas – no idea why they seem to help, but they do – and wandered round Sainsburys clutching them both. Lee never gets embarrassed – he just tells me to do whatever I need to make myself feel better. That helps a lot too.

TIPS FOR DEALING WITH ANXIETY

Ø **FIND YOUR COPING MECHANISMS.** Different things help different people. When I worked out I had to have some control and routine, it helped me get through the day without living in fear. I had to have a bottle of water and bananas EVERY DAY. This was my coping mechanism; it might sound silly to someone else, but it works for me, which is all that matters. Do what's best for YOU. I find rehydrating and drinking water does help. The banana thing – that might just be me but who knows? – I genuinely think it makes a difference. Maybe it's the potassium, but for me they seem to help balance things out. I used to carry them with me everywhere when I was working full-time at the hospital. But whatever you find works for you, it's always good to be armed with those things you know will help you get through the worst bits.

Ø **BE HONEST ABOUT IT.** It can be difficult to tell people at first; I didn't even tell my sister or my mum. But anxiety is very common and it's much better for them to know you are struggling than trying to hide it on top of everything else. So I tell people: I 100 per cent tell people if I'm in a panic. I will say to them, 'I'm panicking right now. I'm sweating, my heart is beating like crazy. And I just need you to just be super normal with me.' Because I think one thing that I did in the beginning was make an effort NOT to tell anyone, and then I'd sit there in silence and it would take over. That was the hardest thing, but once I did start talking about it – especially with my friends – it made them open up about it as well, which has ended up helping them too. So yes, I think talking about it massively helps and it's enabled me to carry on doing the things I want to, like going on holiday and seeing friends.

⊘ **DON'T WORRY ABOUT WHAT PEOPLE WILL THINK.** I can say, hand on heart, I've never had a negative reaction. In fact completely the opposite. And there's the added bonus that if people know about it then it also means they can help you when you need it. Once I opened up I'd literally tell anyone and everyone if I was struggling, so if I was at work I'd tell every doctor, every nurse, every cleaner. I was still a bloody good nurse and my patients and their parents would never, ever know, but having that safety net around me if I needed it was key and a real comfort. So tell your friends, tell your work colleagues. I've found they can distract me without me even realising it, talking to me, getting me to sort out a cupboard, giving me an extra job so I don't have time to sit down and think about it.

⊘ **KEEP BUSY.** For me, being distracted makes a huge difference. Giving your brain something else to focus on is a massive help, so even if you are not with other people, try to find something to do as a distraction. Being busy has become really important to me. People are always asking whether I take a break or time off and apart from family holidays, I don't. That's not going to work for everyone, but for me, keeping my brain ticking, being active all the time means less space for the anxiety to creep in. Again, it's all about finding what works for you.

TRIGGER POINTS

Another thing that I have found really helpful is trying to identify the triggers for the days when the anxiety is bad. This is what's worked for me:

⊘ **TRACK YOUR CYCLE.** For me I think a lot of it is hormonal. Through keeping a diary I have noticed that often my anxiety gets bad a week after my period, when my hormone levels change. I've tried not to delve too deeply into this because it's all too easy to fall down a rabbit hole where you do nothing apart from read up on chemicals and imbalances – that medical background again – but it is really helpful to keep notes and understand when you're more likely to suffer. That way, you can prepare yourself for it, and start to notice the signs before the symptoms take over. So yes, it's back to planning and organisation again, but that's a small price to pay not to live my whole life in fear. So I document my periods because then I know that if I am panicking I can just look at my calendar and see clearly, *Ah, okay, that's what's going on*. Sounds ridiculously simple, but as a busy working mum it's so easy to lose track of my cycle, and this way I can see at a glance that I am at a particular point and what I am feeling makes sense.

☑ **MAKE NOTES ON WHAT YOU EAT AND DRINK.** You might drink a dozen cups of coffee a day without really realising it, and then wonder why you're really jumpy at bedtime. Again, you may well identify a pattern and it's so much easier to identify when it's there in front of you in black and white. Over the weeks and months it can help you have a much clearer idea of any triggers. You can do the same thing with sleep and activities.

☑ **PLOT THE PANIC!** When I'm panicking I write it down. A little dot on the calendar, panic, panic, panic. But gradually, as I have learned the techniques to cope, I've started to see how those dots are spreading out. That's how I knew things were getting better, which was pretty empowering.

I am finally at a point where I feel I can go out and enjoy life again, and understanding the triggers has made that possible. So I know that if I am out late, Lee will pick me up. Or if I have a couple of drinks then I know exactly when to stop. And if I do get that horrible hangover feeling the next day it's NOT a sign of my body giving up, but it's simply telling me I am dehydrated and I need to drink water and eat some fatty foods. Ten years ago I was in a really bad place, but by understanding it, planning ways to deal with the panic and learning how to overcome it, I am now so much better and happy with my life again.

Preparation has also been useful in situations where I have struggled in in the past. For example, when I got pregnant with Mila, I made notes on things that I had gone through first time round so I knew when I gave birth that was how I was going to feel. Things like, my Caesarean scar hurt for this amount of time. It stayed red for this long. The area felt numb for however long and so on. Talking myself through every bit of the process so that I knew what to expect and was more in control – in that way each pregnancy became a learning journey which helped me through the next one.

It was still tough; I only have about three photos of me pregnant. I had no pregnancy shoots, no baby showers, all because I lived in fear that if I celebrated, it wouldn't happen. I would die. CRAZY thoughts. I am so regretful knowing I won't have another baby and have next to no memories of three pregnancies. I'm so sad I felt like this.

I think it was only as I went on to have Mila and Huds and learned to deal with my anxiety that I properly learned how to enjoy the bonding process rather than fearing it. When Darcy was tiny I felt we had bonded despite everything going on, but it wasn't until I was able to look back that I realised maybe I hadn't done it in the same way as with the other two because I was in a different head space.

For me, the most important thing is to understand that if your anxiety is caused by an irrational fear, the first thing to do is to make it rational. So that's exactly what I do now – I talk myself out of it by breaking down the fear, by dissecting it. If I find myself starting to panic, I will look back at the last 24 hours and ask myself, *What did I have for breakfast? What did I drink last night? How much sleep did I have?* So then I can say, okay, my heart is beating really fast right now, but actually I didn't eat dinner last night, and I didn't drink anything after 4pm. So the first thing I am going to do is have a glass of water, and then I'm going to eat a banana (yes, bananas again!) and then I am going to sit down for a few minutes.

It can be hard for others to understand it simply because it is irrational. Lee is the most supportive person you could ever wish for, but at the beginning he didn't get it at all. I'd say I was panicking and he'd be like, 'About what? Your life's great, you've got a beautiful baby and a lovely home ...' But that's just it. It's not rational. And when you've got that fear, you've got that fear, so it's about learning to calm that down. Yes, your heart may be racing and you may have broken out in a cold sweat or be trembling or shaking. But that's a normal fight or flight response, your body trying to help you rather than let you down.

ANXIETY AND BUSINESS

People ask me all the time whether having anxiety has made it harder to start a successful business, and the honest answer is no, not at all, because it's a major distraction and that's one of the things that really works for me.

Yes, running a business can be stressful, but that stress is very different from anxiety or panic attacks. Of course it bothers me if things go wrong, or if a shipment is late and there are going to be delays. But those things are what they are. I know what's happening, I understand what's happening. The order is stuck and will get here when it gets here. I can work around that. Those frustrations are very different from the fears that I can't control.

And actually there are things about it which really help. Doing something you love is always good. And then there's the organisational side too, which has appealed to me in every job I've done. There was nothing I loved more than sorting out the cupboards on the wards, or filling out paperwork with every box ticked, every 'i' dotted, every 't' crossed.

I'm always happy to talk about having anxiety and still being successful, to show how it is possible, and that it doesn't define you. It's a part of your journey and it's how you tap into it that matters. I've found people want to know about it because if they're also feeling that way it is relatable to hear about others going through a similar thing. It also helps show them that there *can* be a way through and they can find their own success.

The Label Lady (and What It's Taught Me)

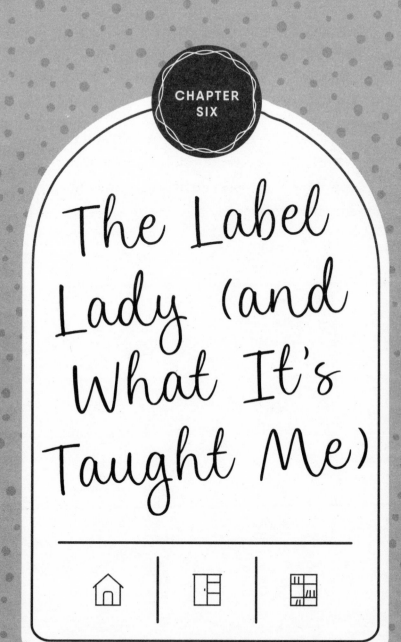

How did I end up becoming The Label Lady? I've always had little businesses on the side, but nothing anywhere near this scale until now. I think the journey probably began when I was promoted to a new role at work. I found the politics overwhelming, so in October 2019 I stepped away from my full-time job in paediatric nursing. I still worked bank shifts but I was looking for a change of direction within my career and wanted to have time to explore options and go for job interviews. This meant that suddenly I was at home more than I had been, and so had more time to sort things out around the house – I have always been obsessed with sorting things out – and then I started doing it to help other people too. So I'd organise things for them and over a few months, it just started to settle in and settle in and settle in. And my family kept saying, 'You love this. Why don't you do this as a job? Organisation is huge at the minute, do it!' And I thought, *Why not?*

As well as my nursing shifts, I had also been running an events business on the side, and because of this I had a computer and a label machine at home. So I just thought, *I could try and make some labels and I guess I could try and sell them and see how it goes.* At that point, I just honestly thought I'd be making a few labels here and there, not creating an amazing business with hundreds of thousands of followers.

I think in all truthfulness, before lockdown happened we were in a world that never seemed to stay still. One minute we were whizzing around, living at such a fast pace, and then suddenly we were stuck at home and surrounded by things that we would normally look at without actually seeing them; you'd open your cupboards each day in a hurry to go and get your breakfast before work and shut them again and walk out. But suddenly we were in a situation where we were opening those cupboards three or four times during the day, and getting quite frustrated with what was in front of us. A mess is one thing when you never actually have to look at it! But if you're stuck at home you're suddenly confronted by that day in and day out and more likely to want to do something about it. It's really easy to think, *I don't want to go in there because it's so messy*, or *I don't want to open that cupboard because I don't know where anything is*, but when there is nowhere else to go and you're surrounded by them all the time, you look at them with new eyes.

Say you like cooking but all your stuff is all over the place – you're going to think *I just can't be bothered* because it means hunting for things and digging through piles of stuff and then stuffing it back in there when you've finished. It's time consuming when it doesn't need to be and adds a layer of stress you don't need. But if all your pots and pans are in one place and your utensils are in one place and your knives and forks are in one place, you're going to know where everything is and using it suddenly becomes more practical and enjoyable.

So that was all part of it, but boredom was definitely a factor too. During the lockdowns, organisation ended up almost being a relief – like you've got something to do that's aesthetically pleasing, that makes sense, something that gives a bit of structure, a bit of routine and control and something that you can be proud of at the end. So I feel like it ticked so many boxes, that it appealed to so many different people at that time and beyond.

The reaction to the business has been really positive. I love the way that it feels like my followers are almost proud of what I've achieved. My friends and family are too, which means a lot. They've always known that I'm a go-getter and I will always try things and so they're pleased that I gave it a go and have got to where I am today. I think throughout my whole life I've striven to hear that they are proud of what I've done. I guess it gives me a pat on the back, a sense of achievement, or self-validation. I've never been massively needy for stuff like that. I don't need a million people to say, 'Oh God, you're amazing'. But it is nice when the people closest to you say you've done a good job, because they can be your harshest critics. So if the people who are always prepared to tell you the truth tell you stuff like that, then you feel, well, I must have done all right.

I also I think it's quite a nice thing to see someone really enjoying their job, so that definitely helps too. I *want* to do what I'm doing. I love doing it; and I think that if you're happy in what you're doing, it shows. I don't get up in the morning and think, *Oh my God, I've got to go to work*. I get up in the morning and think, *Right, I'm off to work*. It's a completely different mindset and I think that shift is really important. I have lots of friends who keep talking about how much they hate their jobs. They earn a lot of money but they're really not happy, though they often feel they've got to stick with it anyway. I find that really sad because I AM happy now, and given the number of jobs I've had over the years, that stands for a lot. Of course, I understand that sometimes you have to be in a job you're not happy with simply because you need to work, but if there's a choice, being happy in yourself can make such a huge and positive difference. I hope it sets a really good example for my kids.

I also hope that I've given my followers a sense of inspiration. I get a lot of messages from people saying, 'Thank you for showing us that we can do it.' When I talk about a touchy subject or not everything being a happy time, it also seems to strike a chord and I think that relatability matters too. Making people think, *Oh, hang on a minute, she's just a normal person.* Because some people seem to think I've got this giant empire where I'm earning millions and millions of pounds and I just sit on my backside all day and do nothing (yeah, right!). So I like that I can share the reality, the commitment, the hours and the dedication that goes into it. And the reaction to that is really lovely. When I announced I was writing this book, people were really happy for me and I was overwhelmed with such lovely messages.

> What I want more than anything is for people to think: She's achieving what she wants to achieve, so there's no reason I can't do that too.

THE PERSONAL TOUCH

I think a large part of why the business works is because I AM the business. It's a very different entity from, say, a big store where you have no idea who the owner is or a clothing brand where you have no idea who the people are behind it. For The Label Lady it's always been, *This is me, this is what I'm making and this is how it's going to happen.* And I've been there myself for every step of the way. Even now, I'm still here every single day, I'm very much here. And I think that means something.

In terms of what I actually create, I think I've managed to find a place where people can be part of it too. So I don't sell them a jar with a label on. I sell them a jar and a label separately, so they can choose combinations they want and then put them together themselves. So it offers a sense that they can do that too, their cupboard can look like that, their space can be like that and so on. I'm not offering anything too complex or too hard to do. It's not mass market where you think the jars are lovely but actually wish you could have a label that says X, Y or Z instead of the ones that are already on there. You are able to personalise things or even create your own labels so again they're exactly what you need.

Another really important thing is that you can spend as much or as little as you want. My prices start at just two pounds. So if there's just one box or drawer you want to organise, it's not a huge outlay. If you've got a whole room you want to sort then you can save and buy accordingly. So it appeals to a large range of people.

There's also a lot of choice and so I hope there's something for everyone and every occasion. It's hard to say what goes down best because it can vary so much from season to season. Our cold cups might not be such a big thing in the depths of winter, but then personalised Christmas tree baubles are never going to sell in the height of summer. So I change what's available accordingly. But my minimalistic labels and jars and bits like that are timeless and always do really well; they sell all year round so they're a great staple.

Even when I do seasonal stuff that might not necessarily be about organisation, it's about ideas – and my brain is a permanent swirl of ideas. I love finding images and colours, working with other small businesses to come up with new things. Thinking, *Wow, that looks so good there* and then making it happen. But it's a lot of work. By December big brands will already have spring collections ready to go and be on autumn/winter for the following year. Whereas for me it will get to Christmas and I'll start thinking, *Oh my God, it's only six weeks until Valentine's Day*. And it's down to me to come up with plans for that. I'm definitely not in the position where I'm planning a year in advance yet, but I think that comes with growth and with learning and we will get there. It's something I'm definitely pushing to get better at, but you can't instantly be good at everything. That's life!

WHAT I'VE LEARNED ABOUT RUNNING MY OWN BUSINESS

Given I only started during the first lockdown, I have learned a lot in a short time! I have loved running The Label Lady from the very start, but I can't deny that it's genuinely the hardest thing I've ever done in my whole life, the hardest job I've ever had by far. It pulls on levels of stress and anxiety that I've never, ever dealt with before. I've learned that:

1. Very often **PLANS DON'T GO TO PLAN**, which, as you'll know by now, is something that really messes with my brain.

2. That it's really important **TO HAVE PEOPLE AROUND YOU THAT ARE THERE TO SUPPORT YOU**, because when things do happen they're there to help you and lift you up.

3. **THAT YOU HAVE TO TAKE RISKS**, and that risks don't always lead to reward, even though you have to take them. And sometimes things go wrong. And it's then about how you pick that back up and turn it around.

I learned in the very beginning that sounding like little old me from Essex was not going to get me anywhere for some weird reason. People were very judgemental about my accent, but the more I've grown, the more I've felt that this is me, so take me as I am.

158

I've also learned that this experience has been a very good thing for me, even with all the ups and downs. The worst thing that could have happened for me during the lockdowns would have been to sit there with nothing to do. The busier I am, the better it is for my brain, so while yes, absolutely, there are lots of stresses, in other ways it helps my anxiety because I'm always on the go.

IT'S A FAMILY AFFAIR

When you run a small business (or have any interest or hobby that takes up time and space), it can be really hard to separate it from family life. I can hold up my hand and say in the early days of The Label Lady this was horrendous because I was doing it from home and it was literally taking over my whole house. I have very little storage at the best of times, so you can only imagine what it was like with three kids, a business, machines, stock and the rest of it. Stuff was everywhere. And I mean *everywhere*.

Now we have the HQ I can at least shut the door on it to a greater extent. I do still take things home but not in a way that it completely takes over any more; after all I can't take everything home. Before that, when I was surrounded by it all 24/7, it was too easy to think, *I'll just do this, I'll just work til two in the morning because all we have to do at the end of it is go upstairs*. I admit I do still pull those late shifts now as well but definitely nowhere near as much as I was doing then.

Back then, we had boxes everywhere, my house was crazy messy all the time because I had stock coming in day in, day out, there was nowhere to put anything and definitely no little places of calm! We had no choice but to work around it. My dining table became my production table and so we had to eat dinner off the kitchen side or in the front room. But the kids have always been great about it – they're kids and I think they're pretty resilient and they didn't care. I do think that the fact that a lot of it was in lockdown actually did us a favour in some ways – we *couldn't* go out so they didn't complain that we weren't taking them anywhere.

Then in the autumn of 2020, Lee built me a shed (aka the den) in the garden and that definitely helped with the chaos. We couldn't fit everything in there, but most of it at least, which felt amazing. The only trouble was that we were still effectively at home, so that whole separation thing continued to be an issue. So I spent many nights sleeping in there and we'd take the kids down to the den for sleepovers. They'd settle under the table; we'd put blankets over them to create a little den and they'd watch a movie and fall asleep. It was like an adventure for them and we'd be there working till three or four in the morning, catching up with orders. There'd be times when I would literally work the whole night down there, then I'd go on Instagram and be like, 'I have just finished', looking like goodness knows what. Because I was so grateful for the work, so thrilled about all these orders coming in. I wasn't giving up, no matter what it took. At the start I obviously couldn't afford to have people working for me, so it was just me and Lee. But I just wanted people to realise how grateful I was and how hard I was willing to work in that situation.

Even if what you're doing is a hobby rather than a business, I do believe that an element of separation is key. In the beginning, for me, my biggest struggle was that I couldn't get ready or have dinner without there being an order or a set of labels or an envelope in front of me. I couldn't keep it separate and that can be really draining on a family. It's almost like you're living two lives in one and you can never get away from it physically or emotionally. Even when we were allowed out and would take the kids to the park I'd have this immense guilt that the house was full of stuff that I wasn't dealing with. So I think it's really important to have that separation and also find some form of compromise too. Involving the kids and Lee allowed them to see and understand it all, so I'd often say 'come on, let's get this done and then we can go and do that'.

Moving into the HQ was life changing. We had space! At least until we got our first shipping container and then it was like – argh, no more room again and we had to take on another unit. But it all works so much better now.

THE JOY OF LABELS

Why do my labels bring joy? Well, for starters, they look great! But actually a lot of it is about helping everything have a place and a plan. I think it's great that you can look at a box or tub or drawer and know immediately what's in it, or you open a cupboard and it's all there. And then for me it just started to build and after that it became about the aesthetic as well. But functionality always comes first; if it's not functional there's no point to it. There's no point having a label for something you're never going to use; it should be stuff that you're using and doing and needing and wanting.

And you can use them pretty much anywhere and everywhere. I don't recommend using my labels on clothing because it's not that sort of vinyl, but any hard surface works brilliantly, which is great for pretty much all areas of the home.

It's really easy for people to say, 'Why do you need a label anyway? It's in a clear container so you can see what's in there.' But actually, when it's run out or gone you can't and so knowing at a glance what you need to replenish is not so simple. When you do your shopping and you think about what you use every day or what you need every day, to have the answer visually in front of you makes an enormous difference.

Labels can save you money too. If I think of my cupboards and the things that we get through frequently, such as pasta, rice, oats, etc. when I'm writing my shopping list I want to know immediately what I've got and what I need more of. If it's all a jumble and you're not sure what's in which packet or tub or how much is left in the bag (or where the bag is if it's crammed behind a whole load of other things), then you can end up buying stuff you've already got, which is an unnecessary expense and is likely to lead to food waste too. When it's all in labelled jars (or containers or areas or baskets) you can see what's there and the labels almost do the next job for you, because it's clear what you need or don't need.

I sell labels for twelve different types of pasta, because people love a bit of macaroni, a bit of fusilli, a bit of penne, a bit of spaghetti for different dishes. And this makes it so easy to see what you've got and what you haven't got, so when you go to the supermarket you don't have to dither over whether you need a little bag or a giant bag – you'll know, because it's in a jar, it's labelled and it's clear. In this way you can really start to organise how much and how often you buy things.

One of my biggest sellers is my spice jar set. You might wonder why, given the jars you buy the spices in have labels on them already. But basically what I've designed is a station that not only looks good, but displays the jars in a way that you can see clearly what's in them, and stops them being chucked in a cupboard in a mishmash where it's impossible to see what's where. The original jars the spices come in are fully recyclable so you're not creating waste, and it also allows you to save money by buying in bulk and decanting. In the set you've got twelve jars, and, whatever you put in them, the contents are clearly visible and labelled. So you can see exactly what you need more of and top up as you go. The days of your cupboard being stuffed with six jars of paprika – because you can't see it at a glance so can't remember if you have any and keep buying more – are over!

But labels are not just about organising the cupboards in your kitchen or bathroom. There are many other places and ways they can be really helpful. For example, they are also very popular with people who might need help in certain areas, so I regularly get people ordering them for relatives suffering from dementia and things like that. They'll buy a label with something such as 'mum's glasses' and put it on the glasses case so that then every time that person sees it, they read it, even if they don't know what that item is just by looking. I have a lot of people who order for children with loads of medication needs, so they might need different things on different days of the week or different types of medication. Or when everyone puts their rubbish out and the bin men have been and suddenly it's *Hmmm, which one belongs to which house?* if you have a bin label with your door number and your road on it, you can make sure you get the right one back. There's such a variety of uses.

And then there are the fun labels too. The decals for Christmas or Easter. The baubles (I love the baubles! I'd wanted to do them from day one). The labels with bright colours or pictures. Once, a customer ordered a fun message to put on her letterbox and that got me thinking so I adapted that message into the style that I do and now there are thousands of doors all around the UK that say, *Oh hello*. I get so many messages from people who've spotted them. I even hear from postmen who say, 'I delivered to an *Oh hello* door today!'

WORKING WITH LORD SUGAR

It all started with an email! I followed Lord Sugar on Twitter and had seen that sometimes he would put out tweets saying that if you were a small business and you were looking for investment then come forward. I'd seen it a couple of times before and never thought anything of it but then I thought, *Why not?* So I sent the email. I remember talking to my sister and saying, 'I don't know if I should be doing this, he's just going to laugh at me'. But he didn't!

Because this was all during Covid, everything was via email and online and we had to have any meetings on Zoom. As you can imagine, it was quite a rigorous process – a bit like being on *The Apprentice* but without the cameras (but yes, he is exactly like he is on the telly!) We had to show everything we'd done, everything we were doing, where our costs lay and so on. It was pretty daunting, but then it was a legal proceeding so it had to be. Everything had to be done over a certain time period. And then it was down to whether he'd choose to invest – which he did, and it all went through in January 2021.

The financial side of the investment was great, but even better for me was the expertise that was on offer as part of the deal. Knowing that there was a team of people I could call on to help me with certain things. 'How do I go about this? What's the correct way to do that? What does this mean?' Teaching me stuff I will be able to use for ever. And of course they have access to other businesses who I've met up with along the way, so it almost becomes a little network. You can use it as much or as little as you need – he basically says, 'if you need us, we're here, so reach out'. That's something money can't buy. I'm quite an independent and stubborn person but I do pick up the phone and it's been invaluable in areas I was unfamiliar with. For example, when I moved over to the HQ and started employing people – I'd never done that before, so they helped me with setting up the payroll and taxes and things I genuinely knew nothing about because I'd never had to think about them before. And obviously I pay pensions and National Insurance now, and all those things I wouldn't have had a clue about from an employer's perspective, and again they were there to guide me through it. When I was doing my first shipment they taught me how to import goods and liaised with their contacts and suppliers to help aid that process and introduce me to that world.

We have board meetings so we meet up and look at profits and margins and what we're doing, what my vision is and everything like that. It's been amazing.

MY SECRET TO SUCCESS

I do think that my honesty has definitely made a difference in terms of where I've got to and what I've achieved. I think that the biggest thing that the corporate world taught me is that I am a human being and that's important. I want people to realise that I don't put make-up on every day. I don't do my hair every day. I'm organised, I love it, but my house still gets messy just like anyone else's. But it's the joy of putting it all back again. My kids are everywhere and anywhere and I think people relate to it. Because I think, as I've said before, on social media and especially Instagram, you see these perfect houses and situations and people going on holiday all the time and you sit there and think, *Why is that not happening for me?* So I wanted people to relate to me and think *There's a girl who works her bum off and is completely normal like the rest of us, and she's doing well.*

I think what resonates most and keeps customers happy is positivity. There will always be good days and not-so-good days but I really try to be positive even when things go wrong. I think that positivity is sometimes what helps other people who are struggling to get through. Though don't get me wrong, there are times I've literally sat on the floor crying my eyes out because I was thinking *I don't know what to do right now*. I had one incident involving a specific colour of vinyl. And I ordered it not knowing that it had been discontinued and they'd brought in a slightly different colour – the name was the same but had one letter different on the end, which I hadn't spotted. I was a regular customer so assumed they would have sent me an email or something, but nothing came and I kept ordering and ordering and ordering and wondering why they kept sending me the wrong colour and they kept saying it was the right colour and exactly what I'd ordered ... And I had hundreds and hundreds of orders to get out and was despairing with no idea what to do. It was a very specific colour and there was nowhere else you could get it from. So I sat there on the floor asking myself *Why am I even doing this?* and worrying about all the people I was going to have to let down. But you know what? I got through it. I rang up the supplier and eventually we worked out what had happened. They had a load of the discontinued rolls they were able to sell us in bulk. And the orders got sorted.

So yes, like anyone else I have my moments, but most of the time I am a pretty positive person. I like to think that I inspire others to want to carry on with their own projects, so I'm forever trying to empower people to do things, empower people to take chances, take risks, and to know that it's okay if it doesn't work out, because there's always something else. There's always a light somewhere, you've just got to find what tunnel it's in.

Another thing that's key is getting feedback and being able to take it well. I always say to people, if I'm doing something wrong or if something's not good enough or needs to be better, tell me. I'll happily take it because I only ever want to do good. If I can change something to improve it then I'm happy to do that and work on it until it's right.

There have been times when the girls will say to me, 'Jemma, that label is shit. We can't cut it properly, it's a pain to pick, it doesn't work.' I've made it and thought I really like it and it looks really pretty. But that's not always enough. It needs to be practical too and if it's not we can't carry on with it, so we ditch it and move on.

I'll never forget once near the beginning when I was doing some back-to-school stuff. I did these little people and they had eyes the size of pin pricks, so every time you peeled the face off, the eyes would go with it and we'd have to reapply these blooming eyes on these glasses every single time. My next-door neighbour ended up helping me during the lockdown summer; she was at home, I was at home, we weren't allowed to mix (or even meet) but her dad was chatting to Lee on the phone and mentioned she had lost her current job. She was stuck at home and I was super busy and needed another pair of hands. The solution? I'd dangle the work over the fence for her to pick up later and we'd discuss it all over WhatsApp. It worked really well even though we never actually saw one another. But with those particular labels the first thing she said was,

'Jemma, I can't do these eyes, they're ridiculous'. I had to apologise as we'd already sold so many, and quickly take it off the website. But while we fulfilled the orders we had already had, it was a complete pain. So it's about listening and learning. It's always essential.

In fact I really did learn from that one because that's how I broke my leg! The fence between us was six feet high so I climbed up onto the wall so I could reach to lower the stuff over. It was a chilly night and when I stepped back down onto our polished concrete table (to avoid the fish pond by the wall) I slipped. I've never actually told anyone that's how it happened until now because I was so embarrassed. Such a silly thing to do. I had to army crawl to the back door and bang for help. I have never felt pain like it.

There's always a light somewhere, you've just got to find which tunnel it's in.

LANGUAGE LESSONS

Whatever you do – in business or in life – I think that finding the right (and most appropriate) words for the right occasion or situation is key.

I have a nursing diploma and a medical background, but I'm not an academic or into medical jargon. So often I would be looking after children and a doctor would come in and I'd watch the poor parents looking completely lost and wondering what he had just said to them. So afterwards I would always tell them not to worry, and explain it in a way that was simple to understand. You can throw terminology around but take anxiety as an example; it can already make you feel like you're not clever enough or worthy or that you don't understand what's going on around you, so using language like that will simply make it worse. But if someone just turns around and says to you, 'Do you feel like your heart is being stamped on right now? Or like you're getting twisted into a knot every time you swallow because you can't get enough air?' Then people get it. It's about making it relatable, and that's something I have found to be really important. In medicine and in business, language can be used to exclude when things could so easily be explained simply and clearly instead. It doesn't mean the person being explained to is thick or stupid, but it can be a way of exerting authority when it really isn't necessary.

In the same way, I have been judged on the way I talk, which is incredibly patronising. There was a time when I was looking for a specific machine for the business. I didn't know what it was called but I knew what I wanted it to do. So I was on Google trying to research all these machines, ringing manufacturers and trying to find out more, such as did I need to buy them complete from other people and bring them in? Did I need to make them myself using various components? I eventually found a company that sold similar machines to the ones that we've got now, and I said to the guy, 'Can you tell me how much they are?' And he said 'They're about £15,000, but don't worry about that' – then didn't even ask me about my situation, my background, anything. I told him that I really want to make X, Y, and Z and this is how I want to do it, and asked about whether the machines could cope with that. And all he said was, 'Okay, thank you for calling us, I'll put you through to our finance team and they can talk to you about if you can get credit or not'. And I said, 'I don't want to get credit.' I was brought up to save for the things I wanted and I don't ever want to see myself in debt, so that was how I wanted to approach my business as well. His reply? 'Oh, so is Daddy going to buy it for you?' This was a *supplier*. I couldn't believe it. So I told him I was confused about why we were having this conversation, and asked whether it was because of the way I sound. And he was like, 'No, no, it's just that you've come in telling me that you want to buy a fifteen grand machine.' I said, 'I don't care if I'm coming in telling you I want to buy a hundred grand machine. I've been searching for months and months to find something suitable and I am desperate to buy it for my business. And you're telling me I'm not good enough to buy it because I need a finance agreement or my dad to buy it for me?' Maybe I did need finance, but why was I so judged?

Obviously I didn't buy it from him in the end, but I have found this happens a lot. When I was looking for a unit for our HQ I got asked 'Are you sure you can afford this? I'm not judging you, but are you sure?' The point was they were judging me – either by my accent or by the way I look, or by the fact I'm young and female and I don't put on airs and graces. I am only ever going to be myself and I think that's really essential. But sometimes it's hard for people high up in business or in the corporate world to handle that. When I go to board meetings with Lord Sugar, I don't wear a suit. I want him to accept me as I am, and he does. It's about instilling confidence in people that I know what I am doing, and breaking that barrier of judgement.

MY BUSINESS TAKE AWAYS

⊘ **NEVER GIVE UP, AND BELIEVE IN YOURSELF.** And believing in yourself is so important. Part of it comes back to the whole 'don't compare yourself with others' thing, which can lead to your self-esteem plummeting downwards and only makes it harder on you. This is about YOU and not someone else. Talk to other people too. It's easy to think that you're the only one who is working really hard and not getting anywhere. Knowing that there are others in the same position can be really comforting and also empowering. It's about reminding yourself that you are capable of achieving the things you want. Some of the things that sell really well on the site are positive affirmations that you can stick onto mirrors or wherever else you like. I love them; I think there's nothing better than a tiny little saying or something that you can look at and think, *Yes, so true*. We all need those reminders. I put them in the kids' rooms too. Try places where you might see them when you're getting ready.

They say things like, 'you are enough' or 'create your own sunshine' or 'never fully dressed without a smile'.

☑ **KNOW YOUR WORTH.** The trickiest thing to charge someone for is your time. Labour is the most costly part of my business and it's the hardest thing to show. Who judges what your time is worth or how valuable it is? I've had the odd person say that my labels are expensive and they get can something else for 20p cheaper from elsewhere. But I'll always say that's fine, I'm not prepared or able to work for any less because it takes me X amount of time and I have so many outgoings and other things I need to pay for. I have to make it worthwhile for me too. Part of me sharing the good, the bad and the ugly is because I want my customers to see how hard I work to provide them with the best service I can, and that's part of the reason why I cost my items as I do. If anyone saw what goes into each and every part of the process, I think they'd absolutely appreciate the amount of work and effort that entails. Yes, we have machines to do some things, but we still have to do so much by hand. Everyone who works at the HQ cares so much about the products. They really are made with love.

☑ **RESEARCH EVERYTHING.** Ask as many questions as you can, and use all the resources we have online. I'd spend hours every day watching YouTube videos on computer software, and machinery. I'd test every item on friends and family and ask 'What do you think about this, what do you think about that, what colours do you like, what colours don't you like?' They are my harshest critics, and if I've come up with a rubbish idea I need them to be open and honest so I can keep trying until I get it right. I test a lot of labels on my sister and that's because she's so busy and so in and out that I know those labels will get used and played with and picked at and put in the dishwasher by accident, things like that. Product testing is important so it's really useful. In the beginning, when I made *anything* I'd show it to all of my family.

CHAPTER
SEVEN

How to
Achieve the
Things You
Want

I think I've always been a goal-focused kind of person, though I think my interpretation of what goals are may be different from others'. For some a goal is a lofty ambition that they may or may not reach. For me it's a task – or set of tasks – that you set yourself to complete.

So when I'm at the HQ, my goal might be to complete 20 orders. When I was nursing, a goal might have been to have every single piece of paper I had done for that day finished and ticked off before I needed to leave. When I was younger, it might have been getting all my homework done, or getting all my books covered. So in that way, I think I've always been 100% goal focused.

None of these may sound like huge things, but it makes sense if you see them as stepping stones – necessary steps to complete to get you to where you want to end up. So there may be a whole list of goals on the way to reaching an ultimate ambition. But they really help and make getting there far more manageable.

Having ambition is a good thing, of course, but setting ginormous goals without breaking down the how and the why can be counter-productive. If they don't happen you can feel humungously let down, or like you're a rubbish person. If you've set smaller goals along the way to the same end, even if you don't get there you can still have a sense of achievement and progress.

I'll be honest. I wanted my company to make a million pounds in a year. And it hasn't (yet!) But then I took a step back and thought, *Why are you doing this to yourself? How hard do you have to work to make a million pounds? It's not realistic at this stage. So stop.* That was the perfect reminder that sometimes trying to make enormous goals can make you feel worse. There are times when you have to give yourself a talking to, to stop feeling sorry for yourself and look at what you can change. What can you bring to the table? What can you think or do or say that will make your day different and make things change? So this year, when we didn't do as well as I'd hoped we would – and I'd put a lot of emphasis on that – I spoke to my family about it and they reminded me that I'd expanded. I'd bought stock that

I'd never have been able to buy before. And I'd taken on two new units that I wouldn't have been able to consider before. So actually, instead of thinking about what I hadn't done, I focused on what I had achieved and that totally shifted my mindset. More often than not, you've done far more than you realise. And that's why having a list where you can tick off your achievements and goals is such a good thing. When you get to the end of the year you can look back at them and be like, *Hang on, I wasn't feeling very empowered, but actually, look at all the things that I've done*. It's a sure way to feel good about yourself.

So if you've put yourself in that position where you find you're not meeting the goals you've set, take a step back and have a look at what they are and think again about what you can do to move in the right direction. Bring it back to the beginning and don't jump too far ahead in one step, which is essentially like trying to get upstairs without climbing the staircase. Without those steps, you don't grow.

I know some people talk about manifestation and mood boards, but when they say things like, 'I drew it on a piece of paper and it came true that year', I personally think that can be quite a dangerous game to play. It gives you an unrealistic sense of what might happen and then you're left with crushing disappointment when it doesn't. I mean, I'm sure I could stick some really nice objects down on a piece of paper. I could work my absolute butt off. But that doesn't mean I'm going to get those things. For starters, it depends on your job, your situation, your family, where you are in life, what you're already paying out for. So you see people talking about how they put on paper that at the start of the year they would have a Range Rover, a massive house and be a millionaire. But if you're someone who's working Monday to Friday in a nine-to-five job, you might try that and then think *Well, that didn't happen for me*. And that's because it wasn't a realistic goal in the first place (there's a big difference between goals and dreams or fantasies!) So take it back to where YOU are. If you're working in a nine-to-five, ask yourself: are you happy? Does it support your family? Can you pay the mortgage? If the answers to those questions are yes, then it's a good place to be. Don't feel the pressure to live up to other people's dreams. Remember, it's about you and your happiness.

I think as a society there's a danger that we get so caught up in materialism that we start to think that our goals are almost not good enough. We all do it. I look at people sometimes and think, *How do you do that? I'm exhausted and I work so hard, so why have I not got there?* It's so easy to do. But then I pull it back and say to myself, *Hang on a minute, what have I got? I'm so privileged. I'm so lucky.* I mean, I have worked for everything I've got, but my goodness, I must never take for granted what position I'm in. Just because I'm not in the same place as somebody else doesn't mean it's not a great place to be. It's important to make goals for *ourselves* and not compare them with others all the time.

Again it's about differentiating between goals, i.e. something you're going to get to or complete; ambition, i.e. something you are ultimately striving for; and fantasy, i.e. the dreams which we all like to have but are mostly just dreams. I mean, I might become an Olympic skier one day, but somehow I just can't see it.

Ambitions are a great thing, though you should try to focus on them with your eyes open. Taking social media as an example, you might look at an account with hundreds of thousands of followers on Instagram and think, *That's what I want*. Which is fine, of course, but you also need to ask yourself if you want all the things that go with that if you achieve that ambition. Will you be happy when your following is that big? When you'll never be able to switch off? When you are likely to get picked on and poked at – because yes, it happens. Or get trolled? It's not just about whether that ambition is realistic and something that you can achieve. Again, it needs to be right for YOU. That's really important. (Also, followers doesn't equal sales or engagement!)

HOW TO SET GOALS

The principle I follow is this:

1. Think of something in your life that makes you happy

2. Think about what your ambition is

3. Take that ambition and scale it down to you

4. Don't look too far into the future

Say your ambition was to get a job in publishing and it took you two years longer than you had hoped to achieve it. It can be really dispiriting to aim for something and not succeed over a long period, so to make you carry on, you need to achieve something over that time, otherwise you'll just give up and move on to something else. Making and completing those smaller goals as stepping stones along the way will show you that you are going in the right direction, even if you are yet to get to the end point.

Goals in that particular case might include networking, pinning down exactly what job you want and looking at the best career path to get there, getting work experience if that's feasible and so on. You might think, *I need to read lots of books so I can really understand the market I want to work in,* so an initial goal might be to read ten books, or to analyse trends.

There will always be little hurdles in the way, but it's those hurdles that will pave your path, so make those goals to see you through that, work through them and be proud of them.

In some ways setting goals is a little bit like making a list – and your goal is completing everything on that particular list. So you start with your brain unscramble, you categorise, you write the list and once you've completed your list, that's a goal achieved. I think 'goal' can be a really huge word so it's good to bring it right back down to basics.

You can start a new journey or rejoin later.

If you choose to stop at a goal, that's fine!

Be calm and okay with where you are in life and with what you have achieved.

First goal

Where are you now

Ambition

New Ambition

Rivers may take turns and new streams can form. A life event can lead to a new ambition.

HOW TO SET GOALS

I see goals almost like stepping stones along a river; moments along a journey that signify achievement. You can work on as many goals as you want and it's okay to stop before your ambition too. Remember, its about YOU and your happiness.

PATIENCE MATTERS

Yes, I know I'm a fine one to talk. I'm a very impatient person. I want everything now. I want everything yesterday. I want to get things done straight away. But sometimes that's where things will go wrong and where you can make mistakes. If you rush and don't take the time to work out what's needed or what you're doing or where you are, who you are, then you're far more likely to fail. So pausing to take a step back before you begin is pretty important. Over time I've learned to be a bit more realistic and through that come to terms with the fact that goals are not things you can usually achieve instantly.

Doing up our house is a case in point. We've all seen the transformations on Instagram where someone says 'here's my room', clicks their fingers and there it is, all decorated and perfect. But it's too easy to forget what that actually entails. We did up our girls' bedrooms so they had their own spaces rather than sharing, which they did before. Now bear in mind that only one of the rooms needed a carpet. There was no building work or electricals required. They both wanted plain white walls so it was really just about painting and furniture. Simple right? Um, no. It was all very well me saying we were going to get both rooms done within a week, but the reality was different. We had to buy two new beds – they both wanted doubles (which I was fine with as they will see them through their teenage years) but I hadn't really thought about how much a bed was – and that's before the cost of the mattress that goes on the bed and then there's the bedding and everything else. Factor in desks and mirrors and chairs (they both wanted swing chairs) and suddenly I was like, *Whoa, I can't afford to do this overnight*. So I had to tell myself, hang on, this might take you six months but it is going to happen. So we broke it down into smaller goals to achieve over that period and that way it was so much more manageable. It was actually a good lesson for the kids as well, in terms of learning that smaller steps can still achieve the bigger picture.

What helped me in this scenario was starting by writing down how much everything was going to cost. It came to far more than we'd originally thought and there is no way we could ever have done it in one go, so in the end it took a few months. In 'Insta-world' that's crazy – who can wait four months for someone to do something? I want to see it tomorrow! But in the real world, I think we did pretty well.

When you're planning things out, visuals can help you look at what you're doing and be a bit more realistic about it. There were times when I'd think, *No wonder you're tired, Jemma, no wonder you've got no money at the minute, because you're trying to do everything at once*. And that's just not how life works. It's easy to forget that these things take time and it's not possible or practical to do it all just like that. Well, maybe if you have a lot of money, but for most people, we just need to remember that we might have to wait for the results we want, and that's absolutely fine.

That said, I still think I drive Lee mad sometimes. If we are doing something like decorating or painting he will often tell me to go out for a bit, because otherwise I will make him rush and he'll make mistakes. I know that's my personality trait, and I shouldn't do that. So if I were to offer advice, I'd say try to be patient with whatever task you're doing or if you're doing it on your own, be patient with yourself, be kind to yourself. Take little breaks because sometimes you can end up exhausting yourself trying to keep up with painting a whole room in a day. An exhausted you isn't going to do the best job. It's the same principle in the workplace or at home or with your children. It goes back to taking those breaks, finding those pockets of calm and not being too hard on yourself.

In terms of saving to do things like this to the house, or to go on holiday and so on, I try to start planning as far in advance as possible, as that gives you time to spread the cost. With holidays you're likely to get much better savings that way too. It's not always possible, of course, but where you can, it's a big help.

We had planned to take the kids skiing for ages and we actually ended up booking that fairly last minute, which wasn't ideal. It's not a cheap holiday at the best of times and as Lee had never skied before, I wanted him to try before we committed. We went to stay with my brother in Switzerland and he had the chance to give it a go, and he loved it, so then we decided to book, even though it was only a few weeks before the holiday. But advance planning still made a difference even then; the kids needed ski wear and so on and that all adds up. However, I have a separate account for each of them – not massive savings accounts, I'm not in a position to do that, but accounts linked to my own where I put a bit away for them every month. So when we were finally ready to go skiing, I had the funds to buy all the stuff they needed. It's a bit like the principle of the old-fashioned Christmas clubs, where people would put a bit by every week so they'd have enough at the end of the year for presents and food, etc.

I talk to the kids about money a lot because I want them to understand how much things cost and how long it might take to earn enough to pay for them. So much is online now, the business, savings ... We never have cash in the house so everything's on a card which makes it harder for them to understand the concept of how it all works. Hudson once asked me if I was just going to 'get more money from my Go Henry card' (which is what he calls it) and I don't think he realised that it's not just an endless supply you can tap into whenever you like.

I'm very specific about the way I budget and like to put money aside rather than leaving it all in one place. I prefer to pay bills annually rather than monthly and have timed all the big expenses like insurance, water, etc. to come out in the two months where we don't have to pay council tax (which is paid over ten months rather than twelve).

I find it far too stressful to have twenty odd bills coming out every month. I know some people prefer to spread the cost, but because I've been putting money aside for bills all year, it works for me. You might say, 'But you're paying out money every month anyway, even if it is into your own account, so it's the same thing'? Financially, perhaps, but organisation-wise I'm doing it the way it works best for me. I have one friend who pays her bills *weekly*. I asked her, 'How do you have the energy to deal with them every single week?', but she said she loves it. It's just something she does every Sunday. I guess that sums it up perfectly – it's all about finding the best way for YOU.

DEALING WITH DISAPPOINTMENT

If the goals you've set are realistic, then generally it's more about not achieving them in the time frame you'd hoped that can be disappointing. But if you're still trying, there's no failure there; it might take longer than you want it to but it doesn't mean you won't do it in the end.

If you're unhappy with the way a time frame is panning out, it probably means that something isn't quite right and you need to have a think about what you can change, what you can add or take away and so on – essentially changing the path to reach that goal. Ask yourself what's got in the way? What obstacles have I faced? Then write them down. If I, for example, have set a target of what I want to achieve at work by the end of the month and I haven't reached it, I might initially think *for goodness' sake, why haven't I managed it?* But then my mum might say, 'but Jemma, this happened and that happened ... ' By jotting down all the factors I can think of that might have affected that progress, I will get a much clearer idea of where the problems lie.

My list might read something like:

> *Postal strikes*
> *A member of staff left*
> *Two people were off sick that month*

These are all things that make a difference, but while you're battling on, your brain will literally forget about them. Having them in front of you puts the circumstances in context and makes you realise it's not that the target was an unrealistic goal. Things outside of your control might have made it impossible on this occasion but there is no reason why next month you won't achieve it. If the things on the list are within your control, think about what you can do differently to stop them being an obstacle in future. Being reflective is really helpful as it allows you to say, 'Hang on a minute, that's right. X happened and Y happened or got in the way, but now I can reset that goal'.

So rather than being disappointed that you haven't ticked off a goal by a certain point, use the time to think about how to edit it or how to make changes so you can get around any sticky points next time.

NEVER TOO YOUNG

Setting goals is a great thing at any age. It's something I've done with my kids since they were young. If they want to go out and do something that involves spending money, I'll get them to work out how much they want or need and their goal will be to earn that by picking sheets of labels (letters such as an 'e' or a 'b' need the bits picking out to leave the necessary hole in the middle. It can be a faff, so I will pay them a pound per sheet to do it for me). I'll get them to calculate how many sheets they need to do and that's their goal and it's their decision as to whether they want to reach it or stop where they are. I think setting goals for kids gives them a foundation; I've worked to give my children so much in life nowadays, much more than I ever had, but it's so important to me that they understand how lucky they are.

School sets goals for them too. Our school has scrapped spelling tests because they felt it was putting too much pressure on young children. They were learning the words by rote every week and not focusing on anything else. It didn't really achieve anything as they'd be on to the next sheet and have forgotten the ones they'd already learned by the time they came to use them again. So instead the children have to read a minimum of five times a week. They can read anything, though they prefer them to stick to a book, so they can get practice in reading books in general. They have to write down what they've done in a reading diary and that's their weekly goal. If they don't reach it they will get a comment from the teacher to say they have not met their reading expectation. And what's really important to the school is that this helps put all those spellings in context; they'll learn the meaning of the word and how they work in sentences rather than just how to spell ten random words that they don't necessarily know how to use. This way helps teach them to spell naturally, because they see the words repeated over and over and it gives their learning greater depth.

PROFESSIONAL GOALS

When I worked for the NHS, the goals for progression were all pretty straightforward as I was working within a clear framework. I started as a band five and my next goal was to move to a band six and then a band seven and so on. It's the same in many other careers too – there is a logical progression to follow and you set your goals accordingly; you strive as much as you want to strive and when you're happy and content where you are you'll stay.

And of course, it's good to set goals within any given role too. When I was nursing, my first goal every day would be to put together a medication schedule for my patients. Paediatrics works differently from adult nursing in that they don't have medication rounds at, say, ten, two and six o'clock; instead, with children the medication is often given by the hour. Depending on the level of dependency or care needed, I'd have up to five patients, and if you have five children all on intravenous antibiotics, those meds can be due all over the shop and you've got to manage that. So my first goal of every day was to take a sheet, essentially an A4 piece of paper, marked with the time on it in hours, so eight, nine, ten, eleven, twelve o'clock and so on, and I would go through their notes, their drugs charts, their feeding charts and write down exactly what was needed every single hour so I had a complete plan in front of me.

Working for yourself is a whole new ball game, in terms of goals big and small. There are lots of benefits to being your own boss – flexibility, freedom, the right to make your own decisions, the ability to action those decisions, knowing that you are building something for yourself. Though there are negatives too, of course. People will tell you that even in a nine-to-five job you end up working more than nine to five, but my experience of working for myself is that it ends up being 24/7. You do not stop. Like never. There is no switching off. Even if I leave the country I will still have my laptop with me and I'll still be doing work. It's hard, so hard, but that's the way it is. It's difficult to explain to people how hard it is. They'll say, 'But you're doing so well' and I'll be like, Yes, but I'm so tired, you have no idea.' It can feel quite lonely.

When you're part of a team there are always people around you. When I started The Label Lady, in the beginning it was just me. And that's the case for the majority of small businesses. You're the admin, the accountant, the maker, the person who posts stuff out ... Obviously I had Lee and the family to talk to, but I still felt like it was all on me. And that can feel very isolating. Even now I have a team at the HQ, although I'm 100 per cent part of that team, I'm also not, in the sense that they can put their stuff down at five o'clock and go home and I can't. I'm very much responsible for them, so I feel it's harder to make big decisions which might impact on them. Part of the loneliness comes from knowing that those decisions have consequences for other people. And even if you're on your own, the consequences might affect your family or your home.

When it's your business, if you make mistakes it can be costly – you've got no one to fall back on, no one to blame. If you're the boss and people call in sick, you're the one who has to pick up the slack. There's no one else to cover and when you're a small team you're relying on other people wanting to be there for you.

If you're working for someone else it's their problem. You can shut the door on work when you go home and if there's an issue you can say, 'Let me ask my boss' or 'I'll talk to my manager'. Whereas when you're self-employed *you* are that person. I think I felt less vulnerable when I was employed. I was very good at leaving work at work. I had excellent time-management skills and I thrived off making sure I had a lunch break and could go home on time. My children were at home so that was my goal. I'd looked after other people's children for twelve hours and now it was time to be with my own. It goes without saying that if there was ever an emergency or other problem I'd stay as long as I was needed, but otherwise I handed over and walked out that door. Not something you can do when you run your own business. But there are pros and cons to everything and this is no different.

ENTREPRENEURIAL SPIRIT

There are around five and a half million small businesses in the UK (a small business counts as one with 0–49 employees) which makes up more than 99 per cent of the business population as a whole. So it's not a niche area! But although the number of self-employed women is rising, at the moment only one in three entrepreneurs are women.

I think there are a number of reasons why this is the case. In a heterosexual relationship, it's often men who put themselves forwards to be the providers for their families and go out and get those goals, though this is definitely changing. I think if you have kids there is still a social expectation that the woman will play a bigger role on the home front. But balancing work and family is not always easy – I'm the living proof of that – and not everyone wants the hours and the stress that comes with running a business. As I've said before, there are plenty of advantages to a more traditional nine-to-five career.

Another thing is that I think women are still not always taken seriously. I've had this so many times. My age, my accent, the fact I'm a woman. It drives me mad that if I'm with Lee people will direct the questions to him and I want to say, 'Hang on, this is MY business. Talk to me'. I know so many women who have had this happen – especially when buying a car. It really needs to change.

I think there is still a long way to go before women are spoken about in the same capacity as men as business owners. That's not to say that there aren't plenty of incredible women out there who are smashing the ball out of the park. It's a question of other people's attitudes. As a young woman I find it's hard to make people see you as worthy. Sure, you might not have years of experience but that certainly doesn't mean you don't have the ability.

This is something I really felt as an employee. You're a young woman saying 'Hey, give me a chance. I've got three kids but I promise I'm going to turn up every day and be the very best that I can be.' Yet they'll go for the bloke who might have a bit more experience but isn't offering anything extra, simply because it's the easy option. My experience is that people aren't always prepared to take risks on people like me and that's something I've found very hard.

I give my business my all and I've tried to break the mould in terms of what a successful business owner looks like. My hair and make-up isn't always going to be perfect. I might end up doing Instagram posts from my bed but just because I'm tired doesn't mean I can't do the things I need to. If I need to write emails I'll do it as and when I can. But I hope that mould breaking will help other women to say, 'Actually I can do this with a family, I've just got to do it in a slightly different way'. Me turning up to a board meeting in trainers and jogging bottoms doesn't mean that I haven't sold thousands of pounds' worth of items. It just means that I'm running to the board meeting after being busy in the HQ and before I go and do the school run, pick the kids up, cook them dinner, then go back to the HQ to make sure the team are all right with all their posting and everything and then back home to put the children to bed. It's really important to me to show these dynamics because a lot of women feel that children are an obstacle to professional success – but we *can* get around it. It can be bloody hard, though.

Another thing in terms of mould breaking is that Lee gave up his career to support me and my business. Before I started The Label Lady we were earning about the same amount and he could have turned round to me and said, 'No, Jem, that's a whole income that you're asking me to sacrifice.' But him losing his job during Covid was an opportunity that wasn't going to come along again and it was the only time I could say to him 'Let's try – this could change what we're doing.' I am so grateful to him and proud of him. Lee is not a risk taker; this was a big deal for him.

BECOMING THE BOSS

I heard that 74 per cent of small businesses are just the owner and no staff. So growing mine from being just me and Lee to having our current team has been a real learning curve. I mean, we started in the playroom using the children's art and craft table. I typed up all the invoices by hand. People would write to me with a list of what they wanted and I'd type it up and send it back to confirm, then I'd make it and package it up and send it out. It was all so manual. I remember I had a hundred orders and I rang my sister and said 'What am I going to do?' And she was like, 'You'll be fine'.

My brother helped me build a website and then gradually it all began to come together. My sister-in-law started to help out – remotely because they live in Switzerland – then my neighbour started helping with the picking and stuff like that. And gradually we grew. We got the HQ when we had just started being allowed to mix and then we had to go back to mask wearing and it was all very up and down. But then I took on one person, then two people, then three people … I've lost people along the way and taken on more.

Sometimes I look at myself and think, *I'm in charge of people. ME.* It's a strange feeling but a proud one. It can be scary too. I always say to my team that I feel very responsible for their lives. It's quite a heavy weight on my shoulders but I'll do everything in my power to make sure

I never let them down. Because ultimately without them there's no me, and without me getting orders in there's no job for them. So yes, I do feel that weight on my shoulders. But I also feel like, how cool to say I contribute to the economy? I pay my taxes and all their national insurance, I pay their pensions and their holidays.

The ironic thing is that The Label Lady happened almost by accident. I just started it thinking, *OK, I like doing this, I'll see what happens*. And that turned into *Oh my God, now I need to do this, this and this*. I didn't have any goals because I'd just come out of my job in order to go and find a new one. This was just my interim. I thought I've got my balloon business so maybe I'll make some labels too for a bit. I'll earn some money, I'll do some nursing bank shifts and I'll find a job that I'm happy with.

Leaving my last job was not a decision I took lightly. I loved my job. I loved my place of work. I loved what I was doing. I was young and energetic and wanted to fight for the NHS and create change. But what I found, unfortunately, was that there were too many people above me that were too comfortable in their positions and weren't prepared to accept any change. And I reached a point where I couldn't work in that environment any more. What people don't necessarily realise is that you have your doctors and nurses in one area of the hospital and then in another area this whole team of corporate leaders who dictate how the hospital is run, where the budget goes and how and why things are done.

But the two teams don't talk to each other and this lack of communication is ultimately, in my opinion, the biggest failure of the NHS. It's really sad. You'll watch porters and cleaners and doctors and nurses say 'We need help', or 'This isn't working', or 'I can't take that child because it's not safe as we don't have enough staff tonight. What should I do?' But the communication to deal with these things is not there. The people in the offices don't know how it is on the shop floor, as it were. They don't see the challenges – or maybe they do. I really loved problem solving and troubleshooting and that's what I wanted to do. But that means bringing problems to the table, and when you're earning £100,000 a year and someone brings you problems, you're not necessarily what they want to have around. There were so many middlemen, which I found infuriating and I couldn't work like that. I didn't understand why when you needed an answer you had to send an email to Tim who would then email Donna who would then email Terry and they'd only get back to you Monday to Friday, between nine and five and it would take a week to find out what you needed to know. I didn't get why we couldn't just email Terry in the beginning. Well, actually I did, and maybe that was the problem. I wasn't afraid to say what I thought and action things way quicker than they were actioned before. And you might be reading this thinking, *Well, isn't that a good thing?* The answer is that it is, if you want to make change and filter out things or positions that aren't needed, but if *you* are in one of those positions, you wouldn't want to be filtered out! So I became a problem.

I wanted to build a bridge between the two areas but the politics and everything got too much and I figured I could do more elsewhere. I left that role to find a new one, somewhere that wanted someone like me. I knew I was a good person. I knew my worth. There were situations I endured during my time in management that honestly broke me. I had to reset. But then The Label Lady happened and took off and pulled me away from that. I reckon it was fate. Everything happens for a reason.

MY GOALS NOW ...

... are pretty straightforward. I'd like to streamline the import and export and shipping side of things. And I want to make sure everything at HQ is 100 per cent secure. It takes time to learn who the right people are and who the wrong people are, but I feel like I've got a really good team at the moment. So my aim is to get me out of working 24/7 and for things to run smoothly when I'm not around. So when I'm there I'm a help rather than an essential part. I believe until your business can run without you, there is not a business. It doesn't mean I won't be in all the time, but it would be nice to be able to take my full annual leave entitlement for the first time. Mind you, the girls laugh at me every time I say that, so let's see ...

MY TIPS FOR ANYONE WHO'S THINKING OF STARTING THEIR OWN SMALL BUSINESS

This is something I get asked about A LOT. Of course, I appreciate that running a business is not for everyone, but I think there are useful lessons for life in here regardless.

⊘ REMEMBER THAT YOU ARE YOUR BUSINESS – especially if you're doing it on social media where it's so easy to look at other people's businesses and think, *I want that and it's all going to happen for me overnight.* Don't get me wrong – it could do, but generally that's not the case, so it's not something you should count on. This is about you and your journey.

⊘ WRITE DOWN WHAT YOU WANT OUT OF IT. It's essential to understand what you are hoping to achieve out of your small business. Ask yourself why are you doing it? Is it because you need to do it to make a living, or is it more of a hobby where what you earn is not such an important consideration? Where does your loyalty lie with the business? If you're doing it as a bit of fun, then great, go for it. But if you're doing it because this is what is going to become your livelihood, then be prepared for it to take up a lot of your life. If it is the latter, then ....

☑ **ACCEPT YOU HAVE TO WAVE GOODBYE TO THE NINE TO FIVE.** It's really important to remember that you can't always shut the door at five o'clock and walk away. You just can't.

☑ **STAY WITHIN YOUR MEANS.** It's all too easy to get carried away and think *I'll buy this, I'll buy that, I'll do this, I'll do that* ... but you need to make sure it's working first. I think because of my fear of numbers I've always been very cautious about what I spend or pay out for, what I do myself and what I don't do myself. Unless you've got someone to bail you out (and that's not the case for most of us), don't go too far too fast and invest in things you can't yet afford.

My own initial set-up was relatively cheap. The machine cost about two or three hundred pounds. Paper, a printer, a laptop. I had most of it already so there was no huge investment at the start. Essentially you have to judge your own situation. I was not in a position where I could have said 'I need ten grand's worth of stuff to go and start the business'. We didn't have that sort of money. So I took to something that I could afford to set up. And if you're in a position where you're testing the waters or not quite sure, or want to try this or want to try that, don't buy thousands of pounds' worth of stock that you don't know you're going to sell. Test the market, get a feel for things and start small before you consider upscaling. It's easy to look at things like *Dragon's Den* and start thinking about growing and long-term investment and stuff like that. But that's a TV programme. You haven't seen the years of work they've put in to get to that moment. It's never a good idea to run before you can walk. Don't be afraid to give something a try, but really research it before you invest too much time or money. If you've got an idea, start to map it out and test it before taking the plunge.

Another thing I would advise is to get active on social media if that's how you're selling. Don't fall into thinking that you need to spend loads of money on advertising, especially at the start. Work with what you've got. When Lord Sugar started his business, he was selling out of the back of a van. There was no Instagram where he could pay to promote his stuff. He would have had his mouth and that would have been it. So start by telling people and get your friends to share and build up that way.

There are really useful insights available on social-media sites too. You can find out the demographics of who looks at your feed, what age they are, where they're from, what times they're on your Instagram. You can find out what days people tend to be on your Instagram (or Facebook or Twitter). So use it to your advantage ... okay, the people who visit my page are in this category, so how will my project or idea fit in with them? Ask your followers questions: what they want to see more of, what colours they like, which materials they prefer and so on. And then follow up on that and show them the results.

FINDING A USP

There are a million people doing what a million other people do and that will be the case for ever and a day. If there is one cleaning business, there are a hundred of them. There isn't just one label company, there are dozens of them. There isn't just one place to buy storage jars, there are thousands. Unless you're an inventor who's come up with their own product, what you need to do is find your unique selling point, what YOU are bringing to the table, and use that as a reason for people to come to you. So, for example, Hoovers and Dysons and Sharks are all vacuum cleaners, but they have different technology and offer different benefits, whether that's models that are more portable or lightweight, better on hard floors or carpets, good for picking up pet hair or whatever. It doesn't change the fact that they all have the same broad purpose, but it does offer reasons for buying one rather than another.

For me, I took the idea of selling labels and tried not only to make them the best they can be but also to ensure that they can be used in ways that aren't necessarily available elsewhere. One example is making my minimalistic labels waterproof and available in a number of different colours (as well as the fact you can personalise them). When I sell jars they are not just any jars – I make sure that they are jars that actually fit a whole packet of spaghetti or a whole bag of flour (if you're going to have half-empty packets and boxes all over the place, it kind of defeats the object!) In short, my selling point is that the product does exactly what you need it to within that organising environment.

THE BORING BITS

Paperwork, financial planning and that sort of thing is definitely not the fun or glamorous end of running your own business, but keeping on top of it is absolutely key. A few things that might be dull but are super important:

⊘ BE PREPARED TO PAY TAX. Yes, this sounds obvious, but when you're an employee it's all done for you so you don't have to think about it. Now you really do! Be prepared – it's a killer!

Ø **DON'T FORGET FEES.** You'll pay them when you set up websites, fees for when all of your payments come in, fees for email hosting, and then there's all sorts of insurance to take into account too. Insurance on your business. Cyber insurance. Public liability insurance. Add to that rent for your premises and it all builds up.

Ø **DON'T SPEND EVERYTHING YOU EARN!** Whenever my friends have come to me and said, 'Jemma, I'm thinking of starting a business', the first thing I always tell them is to put 50 per cent of your incomings away. I think it's really easy to see numbers and think, *Ooh, that's exciting* and not realise the consequences of those numbers. So I'll tell them that on my business account I don't even have a bank card. I have a credit card with a very small budget (and it's very small because they don't give big budgets to business) and that's my spending. Anything else is done by my accountant, so they can say yes or no to what I'm paying out for. Otherwise I think it's very easy to get carried away. So you need to pay yourself, you need to reap the rewards but you need to put that 50 per cent away until you've submitted your tax return, so there are no nasty surprises. There's nothing worse than a tax bill that you can't pay – this way, it's all there, ready and waiting. No stress.

AND FINALLY

I think the following are essential both in business and in everyday life too.

- ⊘ **BE KIND TO EVERYONE.** Treat people with the respect you would want to be treated with. I always like the phrase 'kill them with kindness'.

- ⊘ **BE PREPARED TO REFLECT ON YOURSELF.** It sounds like a weird thing to do but you need to be prepared to take (justified and constructive) criticism, and be prepared to have someone say 'you're not very good at this' or 'this could be done better'. Develop a bit of a thick skin, because without it, it can crumble you for sure.

Honesty is the Best Policy

As a child, probably because of the support my family gave me, I was quite confident. Which is interesting because at school I wasn't the popular one, though I was never the unpopular one either. I found a place between the two where I could be myself and didn't feel like I had to do things to get in with the 'in crowd'. I was funny and that really helped but finding that middle ground was massive for me and meant I was happy in myself.

That was definitely a good thing, because school was cut-throat, really cut-throat. I really feel for people who've been through trauma at school because it's absolutely awful. I'm not sure how I escaped it because if anything I was a loser, the biggest loser ever. But somehow I managed and I think it must have been the dad jokes that made people laugh. My dad is hilarious, honestly the funniest man in the whole wide world and luckily some of that got passed down to me because I never had the clothes or all that stuff to make me 'cool', I wasn't pretty and I had this big frizzy hair. I was also really skinny and paranoid about my body hair so I basically used to wear baggy clothes, hide under my frizz and tell lots of jokes. I was a bit like a walking, talking 'Cousin It' throughout my whole school life; I spent those years hiding and covered up so no one could ever see me properly. Yet somehow I managed to get through school fairly unscathed. If you asked people now, they'd probably say I was all right – and I know I was all right, but in the hierarchy of school I was a loser. I seemed to get away with it, though. Or maybe I just thought I did and was oblivious to what people were saying. It's a bit like now, avoiding reading comments on social media. If people are saying things that aren't nice, fine – because mostly I'm not reading them, so I can walk around, as the old expression goes, thinking *My shit don't stink*. That's been great for my mental health because I avoid those unnecessary lows.

BODY CONFIDENCE

This is something – like many – I have really struggled with, in particular my body shape, my hair and my body hair. They have always been massive things for me and while I might have hidden my body away as much as I could at school, I realised that it wasn't something I could do for ever more. I knew I wasn't pretty, I knew I wasn't one of the beautiful girls and there wasn't much I could do about it. And that was okay. But I also didn't want to stand out and my frizzy, curly hair really didn't help. That's why getting GHDs was such a pivotal point for me; I could at least have straight hair like all the other girls. It wasn't until I got to college that I really got over that.

As an adult I've tried to face up to my insecurities and be honest about the way I feel about them. They are part of who I am and there are only limited ways I can do anything about them.

It's been really hard at times. I have always been really skinny, really tiny and my whole life I have had to listen to people saying 'she doesn't eat' or 'she's anorexic' – neither of which have ever been the case. It's just the way I am. I mean, even now, my wrist size is the same as it was when I was twelve. I'm not sure what I'm meant to do about it!

Whenever I try something on I'll ask 'Do I look too skinny in this?' But the difference these days is that it doesn't bother me if the answer is yes. I'll ask for an opinion because I know I'm skinny, but I have also learned that some things suit me better than others and maybe this just isn't one of them. So when I'm asking for your opinion I want to know: does it actually suit my body shape? If so, great, I like it, I'll wear it. But it took me a long time to understand that and to be able to ask that question, and a long time to have the confidence to be fine whatever the answer.

Body image was such a difficult thing for me as a teenager and the excess body hair really didn't help matters at all. After years and years of enduring it and trying bleaching and various other things with not much success, during lockdown I bought myself a home laser kit. And it worked so well on my legs I thought I'd try my arms, which I've been self conscious about my whole life. I was really scared – I thought, what if it goes wrong and they come back worse? But it worked! I went through my clothes and said to Lee, 'I've been with you for seventeen years – and my summer wardrobe has no T-shirts, no vest tops, no dresses without long sleeves'. And I didn't even realise until I finally had the confidence to get my arms out. I know that will sound ridiculous to some people, that I am 34 years of age and until 2022 didn't feel that I could wear dresses and tops that show that part of my body (an arm! A blooming arm!) without having to lie in the sun until the hairs were all bleached, which is what I'd done in the past and obviously only works when you're on holiday. I'd be tanned, the hair would go blonde and I'd feel much more confident. Just not very practical the rest of the time!

Overall, things started to get better as my personality started to evolve. When I got to college I met new people and started to realise I could be everyone's friend. I figured I might not have a boyfriend because no one fancied me, but I had loads of friends. And I stopped worrying and realised I was funny and I could do this.

These days, I am honestly not bothered what other people think. In fact I've got to the point where I'm quite happy to hang out in slippers and pyjamas and don't care who sees. Don't get me wrong – I like make-up, and there's something lovely about dressing up and feeling really good. And who doesn't love the validation when someone tells you how lovely you look? But I'm comfortable in my own skin now too. And I'm lucky that I met someone who is so laid back that hanging in my PJs is not an issue at all!

THINGS WORTH REMEMBERING

Ø Other people are always going to have opinions but **IT'S WHAT YOU THINK THAT MATTERS**. If you're not sure about something then talk to a family member or friend that you trust. If you know they care about you and have only your best interests at heart, then you will also know that any criticism or suggestions are constructive and come from the right place. And if it's not what you wanted to hear, then you know they will support you through it too.

Ø It's important to **BE HONEST WITH PEOPLE** – but in the right way. For example, if you have a friend who tells you she wants to lose weight, it's almost a natural impulse to reply, 'Oh, you don't need to lose weight'. But dismissing her feelings isn't helping her at all. Far better to ask questions such as, 'What's your goal?' 'Where do you want to be?' 'What will make you happy?' and so on. Make the time and effort to do this, because often with body confidence we *don't* talk about it or discuss what the issues are with anybody. So if you say to me, 'I don't want to wear short skirts because I think my thighs are too big' I'd much rather talk to you about why you feel like that and discuss how that can be changed, and what will make you feel better about them. That's so much better than negating their own opinion, telling them it's not valid, even though they're the one who has to wear it.

⊘ **LEARN TO ACCEPT WHAT YOU CAN'T CHANGE.** Sometimes when people make comments about my body or my weight I'll say, 'Let me share more about that because this isn't going to change, whatever you say. So let's actually normalise this. This is who I am and this is what I am. Let's show more of this.' And remember – so many people are not confident about the way they look. It's not just you.

⊘ **FIND WHAT SUITS YOU.** An advert might say you can wear something no matter what size you are, but in the end it should be down to how it makes YOU feel, not how the advert is telling you you should feel. I was with a friend the other day who was trying on dresses for a night out. She was like, 'I've got big boobs and I don't like my knees and I can't wear any of these.' I got her to write a list (see – lists are great in all areas of your life!) with all the do's and don'ts she could think of and said 'Let's work around that. It's not that you can't find the right dress for you and it's not that you won't look beautiful. But all you've got at the front of your brain is the negatives. And if we pull some of those positives over and we find you a dress where you can say, it ticks that box and that box, you're going to feel so much better. Whereas if you just go out and buy a dress that will cover up all the bits you don't like but does nothing to highlight the bits you do, it's still not going to be something that you will be happy with.'

⊘ You can guarantee that you will always remember the one negative comment rather than any number of compliments. (And I do this too!) But try to take a step back and again **FOCUS ON THE POSITIVES**. It will make a huge difference to how you feel. It's a bit like with the dress buying. Push the positives out in front of your negative insecurities. If you work on them then they will start to outshine the negatives. So when I get a comment about being skinny I try to concentrate instead on something I'm happy with instead. So they might say 'You're so thin' and I will think *Yes, but my boobs are pretty good. Arms? Bit nervous about them but have they got hair on? No.* And so on.

⊘ When it comes to comments on social media, **TAKE NEGATIVITY WITH A PINCH OF SALT** (unless it's someone you know – in which case they're not much of a friend if they're doing that sort of thing in public and you really don't need them in your life.) I try to remind myself social media is mostly people I don't know and who don't know me and that they can't form an accurate or honest impression from whatever photo it is they are commenting on. You also don't know if they have an agenda or where they are coming from in their own lives. That's exactly why I have taught myself to ignore and move on. It makes such a positive difference to my mental health to be able to do this.

I'm not going to pretend that it's always easy. I think people would be shocked at some of the messages I receive (which are harder to ignore than comments). Sometimes I feel like asking 'How many times are you going to say these things to me before I have the right of reply?' I am lucky that I am able to laugh at most of it – it's stuff I've dealt with my whole life and I'm used to it (though that in itself is probably not a good thing because I shouldn't have to get used to it). But sometimes I've got to the point where I think, *I'll just play the game with you. If you want to call me out go ahead and call me out.* And then I'll share it (no names obviously) because I think there are a million other girls out there putting up with this stuff and it's always good to know you're not alone. And I get a really positive reaction when I share things like that.

It's too easy for people to say that being skinny or thin is really easy and anyone who's skinny is really lucky. And I'm not lucky! Because what about all the bloody people telling me how ill I am and how I don't eat? Or how I've got an eating disorder or how I look like I'm dead? (Yes, really!)

Never forget that every body – and everybody – is different. Everyone will have their own insecurities and things they're hung up on, no matter how it may seem from the outside. The most important thing is that we talk about it and we find ways to be positive about it too. People are always going to have these areas of self-doubt, but trying to shift the focus onto the good bits can really help. Ultimately, though, it comes down to how *you* feel and you should never be pressured into doing anything you don't want to do. When people talk about 'embracing your body', or say 'if I want to walk around with my belly out then I should be able to', then that's great. But the whole body-positivity thing is not for everybody. If you don't feel comfortable with having your belly out then it's your right not to do that. If you want to flaunt it, great, but for other people covering it up in a way that makes them feel more comfortable is going to be a much better option.

In short, it's your choice – so wear the clothes you want to wear, show the bits you want to show, cover the bits you want to cover. If you want to make a change to your body, that's okay too.

I know some people feel uncomfortable with how open I am about all this, but I think that talking about it is really important in terms of getting the support you need to get through it. Let's say you've been to the doctor and the doctor tells you you're overweight. If you keep that to yourself it becomes something secretive and shameful when it shouldn't be. And you're shutting out the chance of other people being able to help you make positive changes and support you through them. It makes it so much more difficult to move past it. I've learned to be matter of fact about these things and I think people now come to me for that. They say, 'Okay, Jemma, lay it on the line.' And I think for people who are struggling it's good to have someone like that in their life. It's about helping rather than pacifying. There's a big difference.

When it comes to my own children I have tried to instil confidence and positivity in them from an early age. I tell them everyone's different, right? Everyone looks different, everyone sounds different, everyone speaks differently. That is normal – but that is also so beautiful. You don't have to look and sound or want to be exactly like everyone else. In fact if you're that little bit different, you're the one who will stand out in a crowd, which can be a really good thing. If you want to do something in life, people will remember you for not being the same as everyone else, for being that bit more fun, or having that bit more style or whatever else it is. Don't ever feel you need to follow in the mould of every other person. If you're happy in what you're doing and you're not harming anyone then just enjoy being you.

When my children talk to me I try to be open with them as I really want them to learn to be comfortable in their own skin. One example: Mila has tiny bits of eyebrow in the middle. You can barely see it but she was like, 'I've got a unibrow. Everyone is going to laugh at me.' I asked 'Has anyone laughed at you yet?' She said no. So I said to her, 'Listen to me here. It's nothing that we can't fix when you're older, if that's still what you want to do. But right now there's absolutely no reason to touch it. You are beautiful. You are perfect. You are seven years old.'

I also said that as she gets older there may be things about her body or things in her life that she doesn't like. We can talk about them, but there are certain things we can change and certain things that we can't, so we have to learn to love and live with them. But I will always be there to guide her through it. I showed her beautiful girls with big eyebrows and made her feel good. Be proud of yourself and your body – no one else is you.

I've always said to them that if you want to succeed at anything then you have to be happy with yourself as a person. And it's tough for parents these days, we have a battle bringing up our kids with the bad side of social media and all the pressures it can bring. So I think my biggest job is to champion myself and show them that I am comfortable with who I am. So I want them to see me at my worst, but still happy, if that makes sense. I always say to them, 'I want you to know you're beautiful', 'I want you to know you're amazing'. It's so important to me to try and instil that self-belief.

Darcy is my oldest and she's my shy child, though she's not shy with people she knows. But it's hard when it's people she doesn't. Sometimes you've got to be there for them and sometimes you've got to let them learn to get through it themselves, because you're not always going to be there for them. But mostly I want them to be like me in that I was always taught to live life – and to live life happy and grateful for what you have. Of course they are going to learn things along the way – that there will be things they struggle with and things that don't always go right but that they can actually do something about it. So I want them to be confident. It doesn't mean they have to be these huge extroverts that go out and scream from the rooftops, but I do want them to feel confident with meeting people, going out and trying things and knowing that failures are part of that. My girls ice-skate and if they don't win in a competition, the biggest thing I can teach them is okay, they might not have won this time, but what are they going to do before the next competition? You're don't need to be upset about it because that was you trying, so now is the time to pick yourself up and look at what you can do better, how you can try harder or change things next time. It's all about learning from things so that next time is better – again that's a lesson you can apply anywhere in life.

I think it's important to remember that you're never going to succeed at everything, and you need to work for the things you want. I didn't just wake up one day and this happened for me. Though actually ... it kind of did. But it happened because for ten years prior to that I was doing X, Y and Z. So that's what eventually led to me reaching a certain point, and *then* it happened. I guess you could compare it in a way to an athlete winning an Olympic medal. They got there not only because of how they performed on the day, but also because of the hours and months and years of preparation and training they put in to get to the Olympics in the first place. Of course, for some people it might never happen but you can't get caught up in being unhappy about that; you've got to be happy with where you are and as long as you are, wherever that is in your life, then that's all that matters.

We all compare ourselves with other people, and I think that this is something people will continue to do for ever. There's a million people I could compare myself to and think, *Gosh, I wish I was like them. I wish I was like that.* But sometimes you have to remember to bring it back home and think, *What am I? Who am I? What am I doing?* Because ultimately you're the only one who can work on these feelings and learn to appreciate the many things you have going for you.

It's taken me a long time to get to the point I'm at now and I know that there will be people reading this who think it will take them a long time to get to that place too. Maybe it will, maybe it won't, but it will always be worth it.

I've worked really hard on my own anxieties and insecurities, and am happier in my own skin than I have ever been before. But even now there are things I struggle with – we are all human! – and I often find myself nervous about things going wrong or tempting fate. When I held the Christmas party for the HQ team, it was a first for me because I'd always been scared that everything would end, so what would happen if I celebrated something and then lost it all tomorrow? I was the same with baby showers. I never had one – it's funny, I get really worried about things like that. If I'm going on holiday I am scared to think about the fun aspects in case anything happens so we can't go. It's ridiculous but that's how my brain works and it's something I have to deal with.

Interestingly, I never worry about other people doing any of these things. I planned my sister's baby shower without any qualms at all because it wasn't my baby shower. It all comes down to doing what's best for YOU. Don't conform to pressure. I had so many people who kept telling me I needed a baby shower, I needed to do this, I needed to do that, but I stuck to my guns because I didn't feel comfortable in that situation. It doesn't mean I'm a bad person because I chose not to have a baby shower. It doesn't mean I'm not as cool as everyone else. I just didn't feel comfortable having one so I didn't have one and I found the strength to say no.

Since I started The Label Lady my life has changed beyond recognition. Yes, I'm still a busy mum of three, but aside from that – just wow. Sometimes I have to pinch myself. If you'd asked me back in 2019 where I thought I'd be today, I don't think I could even have begun to predict everything that's happened over the last two or three years. There's been so, so much in such a relatively short amount of time. Stepping away from full-time nursing. Starting my own business. Working with my husband and getting the whole family involved. Setting up the HQ. Building a brilliant team of colleagues. Having Lord Sugar as a business partner. Daily interactions with my amazing Instagram followers … It's the stuff of dreams, although it's taken a lot of blood, sweat and tears and I've worked harder than I ever thought possible.

Along the way I've learned so many lessons, which have proved to be invaluable in life as well as business. But if there is one that stands out above the rest, it is never to give up on trying to achieve the things that YOU really want. Believe in yourself, believe you can do them and never let anyone tell you you're not good enough. I'm proud of the business I've built, but I'm even more proud of the fact that when people put me down or told me I wouldn't make it, I proved them wrong. You should never have to hide who you really are to get to where you want to be and I'm glad that I found the courage to understand that and to be myself.

I might be The Label Lady, but at the heart of it all, I'm just a normal girl from Essex. And I'm pretty chuffed with the fact that this Essex girl done good. I hope that by reading this you feel inspired to be you, do you and continue on your own journey.

Thank you

Thank you to my family for always supporting me, no matter how crazy an idea or if it works or not. Just the belief that I would succeed no matter what was exactly what I needed to keep me going. I will never take for granted how close we are as a family and how much love we all share. Even when we drive each other crazy we are always there to support each other no matter what. I hope I have made you all proud of everything I am and have achieved and may we forever continue our bond into our children, and continue to grow old together always. xxx

P.S. I can only imagine you all laughing about how mushy this is coming from me, but it's true! I have a heart ;)

LEE – the person who has stuck by my side through it all. Through the good and the bad, you have always been there. I couldn't imagine having a more amazing person by my side and I just want to say thank you.

Thank you to **MY FRIENDS** for being just that – the ones who make me laugh, the ones who carry my tears, the ones who are there when I need them, always.

Thank you to **THE AMSHOLD TEAM. LORD S** – for believing in my business and your amazing team who have helped me learn so much over the past two years.

Thank you to **MY HQ TEAM.** It's been a ride, that's for sure! From moving out of the Den in the garden to employing the most amazing team to help me make and create labels. Your passion for my passion makes working with you all everything I could ever ask for. I couldn't do it without you all and honestly am so grateful for you all every day.

A special thank you to **AMANDA HARRIS, ELISE MIDDLETON** and **ANNA DIXON** for always being there and listening to my ideas, (including the crazy WhatsApps at all hours and emails in the middle of the night), helping me through this process and believing that I was good enough to do this. You are amazing. x

CHARLOTTE HARDMAN, MICHELLE WARNER and **JASMIN KAUR** on the editorial team. **NAT GONCALVES** and **LUCY BROWN** in the campaigns team. **BECCY JONES** in production. **CHARLOTTE MCDONALD** for copy-editing the book, **EMILY VOLLER** for designing it and **YULIA PYLPCHUK** for her illustrations.

Small Businesses and Instagram Accounts

My sister did a very similar thing and I thought it was such a lovely idea that I would like the to do the same, because without the support of these wonderful accounts around me I wouldn't be where I am today. Thank you all so very much. I love our small-business supports and I promise to always continue to be a small-business champion.

You are all amazing!

SMALL BUSINESSES

PARTIES AND EVENTS

The Little Luxe Event Co
@thelittleluxeeventco

Camping Cinema
@campingcinema

Stylish Teepees and Picnics
@stylishteepeesandpicnics

Bleubell Tents
@bleubelltents

1st Event Luxury Travel
@essexpartybusco

Bonn Events
@bonnevents

Parties & Signs
@partiesandsigns

Six Stories
@sixstories

The Toddler Town Company
@thetoddlertowncompany

ENTERTAINERS

Alice & Jack Acoustic Duo
@aliceandjackduo

The Undercover Waiters
@theundercoverwaiters

Party Monsters
@partymonstersentertainer

Party with Jelly Jade
@partywithjellyjade

Little Party Monkeys
@littlepartymonkeys_

FLOWERS

Big Little Blooms
@biglittleblooms

Broadway Blooms London
@broadwaybloomslondon

Primrose & Ivy
@primroseandivy

Daisy May's Florist
@daisymaysflorist

Elisha's Floral Design
@elishasfloraldesign

Writtle Sunflowers
@writtle_sunflowers

CAKES AND CATERING

Lolly Poppin
@lollypoppin_uk

The Fizzy Drumstick
@the_fizzy_drumstick

Katie Cochran
@golden_whiskgw

Alex Batty
@mascalls_bees

Chef Jonny Mervish
@served_by_merv

Sweet Nellys
@sweetnellysco

Sweet Baked Sensations
@sweet_baked_sensations

Cake Bops
@cake_bops

The Fat Fairy
@the_fat_fairy_

JB Treat Carts
@jbtreatcarts

Sweets in the City
@sweets_in_the_city

Choc Pops
@choc_pops_upminster

Charlotte's Cakes
@_ccakes

Not Sweet Enough
@notsweetenough1

CRAFTS AND STATIONERY

Lulabell Gifts
@lulabellgifts

Love, Daisy
@love.daisyshop

Emma's Ink Pot
@emmasinkpot

Incy
@incybox

Jelly Fabrics
@jellyfabrics

Crayation Station
@crayationstation

Eliza Mac Fabrics
@eliza_mac_fabrics

Ashprint London
@ashprintlondon

Boggledybook
@boggledybook

Perfect Planner Company
@perfectplanner.company

GETAWAYS

Holidays Wales
@holidayswales

Ashlin Farm Barns
@ashlin_farm_barns

HOME DÉCOR

Fall with Grace
@fall_withgrace

Ava May Aromas
@avamayaromas

Lauren Zoe Carter Art
@laurenzcarterart

Knots & Ivy Ltd
@knotsandivy

Village Wax Melts Ltd
@villagewaxmelts

By the Magnolia Tree
@bythemagnoliatree

Pretty Little Home
@pretty_little_home

Deb's Dazzling Designs
@debsdazzling

Crafty Little Pickle
@craftylittlepickle

Moons & Marbles
@moonsandmarbles

Haus of Ven
@hausofven

Garage Style
@garagestyleltd

Hollie's Little Shop
@hollieslittleshop

Bella Bow Fairy
@bellabow_fairy

ILoveRugs
@_iloverugs

Dotty Dolittles
@dottydolittles

Oh So Daisy
@ohsodaisy.shop

A Clarke Carpets & Flooring
@aclarkecarpets_flooring

EssexCrafts94
@essexcrafts94

Fred & Bo
@fredandbo

WatersHaus
@watershaus

Spirit Owl
@spiritowlltd

Levere
@leverehome

Gracie Jaynes
@gracie_jaynes

Forever Framed Gifts
@foreverframedbyemma

Pebbles & Wool by Adele
@pebblesandwool

FASHION

White Ribbon Collection
@whiteribboncollection

Tula Tella Jewellery
@tulatella

Tomm Jewellery
@tommjewellery

I Do Fancy
@idofancyonline

Lisa Bea
@lisabeabags

Happy Ziggy London
@happyziggyldn

Kooky Bloom
@kooky_bloom

Slips n Slides Personalised
@slipsnslidespersonalised

LITTLE ONES

Panda & Pip
@pandaandpip

Busy Boards London
@busyboardslondon

Blossom & Ivy
@blossomandivy_

Mini Fox Clothing
@minifoxclothing

Sew Queenies
@sew_queenie

Squelch Wellies
@squelchwellies

Cublife Clothing
@cublifeclothing_official

Amber & Noah
@amber.andnoah

Sal's Shoes
@salsshoes

Baby & Me Gift Box
@babyandmegiftbox

The Nursery Barn
@thenurserybarn

Little Brown Mouse
@thelittlebrownmouseco

PETS

Poppy + Ted
@popandtedthreads

My.Pawchella
@my.pawchella

HEALTH AND BEAUTY

Laura Cord
@nails_by_lauracord

Pamper Pod
@pamper_pod

Tanya Mobile Hairdresser
@tanya_mobile_hairdresser

The Wrinkly Elephant
@thewrinklyelephantcompany

REHAB.
@rehabyourhair

Luna
@wearelunaapp

Bridies Bombs
@bridies_bombs

Milky Mammas
@milkymammas

Bliss and Aura
@blissandaura

Fox & Moon
@fox_and_moon

Gemma Horner MUA
@gemmahornermua

CLEANING AND ORGANISING

Clean & Tidy Home Show
@cleanandtidyhomeshow

Ovenclean Chigwell Warren
@ovenclean_warren

Dot.
@decant.organise.time

Purdy & Figg
@purdyandfigg

AMAZING ACCOUNTS

LIFESTYLE

Stacey Solomon
@staceysolomon

Sophie Hinchcliffe
@mrshinchhome

Charlotte Greedy
@missgreedyshome

Amy Hart
@amyhartxo

Helen Brown
@zebrawhocankickass

Harriet Waite
@harrygtobe

Me Julieeee
@x_me_julieeee_x

Emily Norris
@mrsemilynorris

Glam Fairy's World
@glamfairysworld

Saira Begum
@sairas_life

David Solomon Photography
@photography_by_david_solomon

INTERIORS

No Place Like Home
@noplacelikehomeinterior

Home with Mrs K
@homewithmrsk

Carly's Home Ideas
@carlyshomeideas

Project Ivel
@project_ivel

At Home with Riri
@athomewithriri

Redbricks Lifestyle
@redbricks_lifestyle

Jen's Gathering Nest
@jensgatheringnest

CLEANING AND ORGANISING

Dilly Carter
@declutterdollies

Sophie Liard
@thefoldinglady

Cleaning with Mario
@cleaningwithmario

My Geordie Home
@my_geordie_home

Hall at Home
@hall_at_home

Sharon Owen
@a-welsh-spring-gleam

The Declutter Hub
@declutterhub

Twinkle Cleaning Duo
@twinklecleaningduo

Clean with Abbi
@cleanwithabbi

Pretty in Pink Squares
@prettyinpinksquares

Mrs Clarke's Cleaning
@mrsclarkescleaning

PARENTING

Not a Fictional Mum
@notafictionalmum

Part Time Working Mummy
@parttimeworkingmummy

BUSINESS AND TECHNOLOGY

Tom Pellereau
@inventor_tom

Alan Sugar
@lord_sugar

Dell
@delluk

Gramersi
@wearegramersi

MONEY

Gemma Bird
@moneymumofficial

HEALTH AND BEAUTY

James Johnson Celebrity Hair
@iamjamesjohnson